The Army of the American Revolution and Its Organizer:

Rudolf Cronau's Biography of Baron von Steuben

Edited by *Don Heinrich Tolzmann*

HERITAGE BOOKS
2011

HERITAGE BOOKS
AN IMPRINT OF HERITAGE BOOKS, INC.

Books, CDs, and more—Worldwide

For our listing of thousands of titles see our website
at
www.HeritageBooks.com

A Facsimile Reprint
Published 2011 by
HERITAGE BOOKS, INC.
Publishing Division
100 Railroad Ave. #104
Westminster, Maryland 21157

Copyright © 1923 R. Cronau

Copyright © 1998 Don Heinrich Tolzmann

— Publisher's Notice —
In reprints such as this, it is often not possible to remove blemishes from the original. We feel the contents of this book warrant its reissue despite these blemishes and hope you will agree and read it with pleasure.

International Standard Book Numbers
Paperbound: 978-0-7884-1066-6
Clothbound: 978-0-7884-8695-1

Editor's Introduction

Rudolf Cronau is certainly a name well known in the field of German-American history. The author of several works, including *German Achievements in America*, Cronau was clearly one of the major German-American historians of the early 20th century. [1] His works were all well researched and illustrated. Then, as now, his works are of value for those interested in German-American history.

This biography of Baron von Steuben was published shortly after the First World War, in 1923, which certainly was a low point in the German-American experience. Cronau saw it as his task to make known the role German-Americans had played in the history of the U.S., and in this particular case, the role that Baron von Steuben had played in the American Revolution. Written in a popular style for the general public, this work provides the basic facts with regard to the contributions made by Baron von Steuben. Moreover, it also provides information on German-American life after World War One, and on the newly formed Steuben Society of America.

For some time, the undersigned has been engaged in the task of illuminating the role that German-Americans have played in the history of this country. In so doing, he has edited a number of works dealing with the American Revolution, including: *German-Americans in the American Revolution: Henry Melchoir Muhlenberg Richards History* (1992) and *German Allied Troops in the American Revolution: J.G. Rosengarten's Survey of German Archives and Sources* (1993). Most recently, the editor has brought out another volume, which will be of assistance in researching German-American involvement in the Revolution: *German-Americana in Europe: Two Guides to Materials Relating to American History in the German, Austrian, and Swiss Archives.* (1997).[2] These and other sources will hopefully draw attention to this chapter of German-American history.

This current work has been edited to further contribute to our understanding of Baron von Steuben, as well as to the field of German-American history in general. Those seeking more recent work on the topic are referred to Margrit B. Krewson, *Von Steuben and the German Contribution to the American Revolution: A Selective Biblioraphy.* (1987).[3]

Notes

1. This was edited by the editor of this volume, and published by Heritage Books, Inc. in 1995.

2. All were published by Heritage Books, Inc.

3. Published by the Library of Congress, Washington, D.C.

Don Heinrich Tolzmann
University of Cincinnati

Major General Baron von Steuben
Organizer of the Army of the American Revolution.

From the original painting by Ralph Earle, now in possession of Mr. Wm. M. Austin, New York.

The Army of the American Revolution and its Organizer.

A Thrilling Story of the times that tried Men's Souls

By Rudolf Cronau

Published by
RUDOLF CRONAU
340 East 198th Street, New York

Copyright, 1923, by R. Cronau
New York

Works by the same Author

America, the History of Its Discovery. 2 vols. with 545 illustrations and 37 maps. (Leipzig 1890-92) Award World's Columbian Exposition.

The Discovery of America and the Landfall of Columbus.
The Last Resting Place of Columbus. Two monographs based on personal investigations. With many maps and illustrations. (New York, 1921.)

Our Wasteful Nation. The story of American prodigality and the abuse of our National Resources. (New York, 1908.)

Three Centuries of German Life in America. With 210 illustrations. (Berlin. 1909.) Award by the University of Chicago.

Woman Triumphant. The story of her struggles for freedom, education and political rights. (New York, 1919.)

Illustrative Cloud Forms for the Guidance of Observers in the Classification of Clouds. (U. S. Publication No. 112, Washington. D. C., 1897.)

and others.

CONTENTS

	Page
Preface	I, II, III
The Arrival of a Distinguished Foreigner in America and His Great Mission	1
In the Winter Camp at Valley Forge	10
Organizing the Revolutionary Army	19
The Battle at Monmouth and the Treason of General Lee	32
Steuben's "Regulations," the First Manual for the American Army	38
Watchful Waiting in the Highlands of the Hudson	48
The Treason of Benedict Arnold	58
Steuben's Eventful Campaign in Virginia	69
Steuben's Part in the Siege of Yorktown	78
The Most Critical Period in American History	83
Disbanding the Revolutionary Army and the Founding of the Society of the Cincinnati	97
Years of Disappointments and Blighted Hopes	110
Cincinnatus Redivivus	122
Steuben's Death and Last Resting Place	128
Posthumus Honors and Appreciations	133
"In Times of Peace prepare for War"—the great but unheeded Lesson of Steuben's Life	140
The Steuben Society of America and its Aims	146

PREFACE.

SINCE the discovery of the New World by Columbus no other event has made such a deep impression on all humanity as the successful founding of the United States of America. The spirit of liberty, proclaimed in those times, spread like wildfire from country to country. It incited the inhabitants of France to revolt against the despotism of their kings; it inspired numerous great men of Central- and South America to follow the example set by the noble fighters in the North and to bring the oppressive rule of Spain in our hemisphere to an end. It found an echo in the similar efforts of the inhabitants of Hayti and Brazil; it encouraged the nations of Europe to struggle for parliamentary governments, and it has moved, in our days, even the Filipinos and Chinese to proclamations, which in their wording, almost imitate our own Declaration for Independence.

In view of these facts the great mission of the United States of America is evident. As long as its citizens maintain their country as "the Land of the Free," as long as its youth in the development of its own character incorporates the virtues of the heroes of the years 1775 to 1783, our United States will remain a model for all other nations.

But during the last thirty years strong efforts have been made and many million dollars have been spent by foreign propagandists to convince our people that the War for Independence was "a most unfortunate blunder without justification," a "grave mistake" that ought to be remedied as soon as possible either by the return of our country into the British Empire or by forming a "British-American Union."

The gradual elimination from our school histories of all reference to the nefarious part played by England in American history; the constant detraction of patriotic men like Washington, Franklin, Jefferson, Hancock, Adams, Henry, and all the other "foolish mutineers" of the War of the Revolution; the movement to ignore the Declaration of Independence and substitute the signing of the British Magna Charta to be celebrated by American youth as the true origin of our liberty, are so many indications whither currents are carrying our people.

Of all the great heroes of our War for Independence no one has been more persistently ignored than Baron FREDERICK WILLIAM VON STEUBEN, the organizer of the Revolutionary Army. The majority of our historians while they compiled voluminous works on the glorious past of our country, devoted little space to this remarkable person. And when we consult the text books placed into the hands of our children in school, we find that they are either silent or confine themselves to mentioning his name, with the remark that he was the drillmaster of Washington's army.

Why is this? Is it because Steuben was not of English origin, but "only an alien"? Or is it that our historians, not well versed in foreign languages, shrank from the difficult task of delving into the 16 volumes of original letters of Steuben and other documents relating to him, written partly in French and partly in German, and now preserved in the archives of the New York Historical Society?

Leaving these questions undecided, we wish, however, to say, that a perusal of these letters and documents is of highest interest to every student of American history, because they give a deeper insight into the real conditions of the times that tried men's souls than can be obtained anywhere else. And by a close investigation of the cold facts such students will realize, that during this eventful period there existed, Washington excepted, no other man who showed such ability, perseverance and devotion to the great cause of liberty than Steuben.

It was he who infused the unorganized bands of defeated and discouraged volunteers and militia men, assembled at Valley Forge, with a sense of discipline as well as of confidence. It was he who converted them into an excellent fighting machine, in many respects superior to that of the enemy, and able to win the victories of Monmouth, Stony Point, Yorktown and other places. In his "Regulations for the Order and Discipline of the Troops of the United States" he provided the officers for the first time with a clear and definite manual for the performance of their duties in connection with troops, their weapons, exercises, marching, camping, maneuvering, signal service, inspection, aid and treatment of the sick and wounded.

Well aware that the future might bring again serious quarrels with foreign nations, Steuben also emphasized that it would be wise in times of peace to prepare for war. He therefore proposed not only the creation of a standing army of regular troops, but also the founding of a regular military institution, the present Military Academy at West Point.

Furthermore Steuben suggested the founding of the "Society of the Cincinnati", the oldest and most distinguished of all hereditary societies in the United States, organized for the purpose of uniting all American generals and officers who had served under Washington, into a union of true friendship and brotherhood.

It may safely be claimed that without Steuben's invaluable assistance, experience and wise counsel the history of our country might perhaps read very differently. It may be that George Washington would have met, like the Irish patriot Roger Casement in our days, an ignoble death in being shot as a rebel; that the Declaration of Independence would have been discarded as a "scrap of paper"; that our War for Independence would have ended in failure, and that, instead of the beautiful Stars and Stripes, the British Union Jack would still float over our coasts and cities. That Washington himself was deeply impressed by the great services rendered by Steuben, appears from the appreciative letter he wrote to his comrade in arms in the very last hour before resigning his commission as Commander-in-Chief.

For all these reasons the fascinating story of Steuben and his achievements must appeal strongly to all who have respect for genuine manhood, efficiency and valour. A knight without fear and without reproach Steuben is one of the most heroic figures in American history.

The Arrival of a Distinguished Foreigner in America and His Great Mission.

It was on the first day of December, 1777, that, after a rough voyage of more than two months the French gun-boat "Flamand" slipped into the harbor of Portsmouth, New Hampshire. The vessel brought to the Americans, who for over a year were engaged in their struggle for liberty, a quantity of military supplies, among them 52 brass cannon, 19 mortars, 22 tons of sulphur and 1,700 pounds of powder, indeed a welcome addition to the scanty resources of these heroic men.

But for some other reasons the arrival of the "Flamand" was for the Americans of greatest importance. There was aboard a party, consisting of the Prussian General Baron Friedrich Wilhelm von Steuben, his secretary Duponceau and his aides De L'Enfant, De Romanai, De Pontiere, and Des Espinieres. They came with the intention to aid the Americans in their great cause.

Before we endeavor to relate Steuben's activities in America, a few notes about his former life and the motives and circumstances that brought him to the New World, are in order.

Born on September the 17th, 1730, at Magdeburg, Germany, as a descendant of a noble family, which for generations had produced soldiers, Steuben led a soldier's life since his seventeenth year. Reared in the rigorous military school of Frederick the Great, he took actual part in many battles of the Seven Years' War, fighting at one time against the Russians, at another against the French or Austrians. He took part in the battles of Kunnersdorf, Prag and Rossbach, in the siege of Schweidnitz, Silesia, was wounded several times, and distinguished himself to such an extent, that he attracted the attention of King Frederick the Great, who appointed him as an aide-de-camp on his personal staff.

Moreover, the king chose him one of the six officers, who were by him personally instructed in the science of war and military tactics. During the last year of the war Steuben was Quartermaster-General and Adjutant-General to the king, and, during the winter of 1762-63 he had command of the regiment Von Salmuth, subsequently Hesse-Cassel.

So Steuben enjoyed exceptional opportunities to familiarize himself with all questions pertaining to warfare: with the drilling and training of soldiers, with the important tasks of providing for and equipping the troops; of securing and caring for arms and ammunition, their inspection and control.

When the Seven Years' War came to an end, Steuben resigned and accepted the position of Grand Marshal at the court of the Prince of Hohenzollern-Hechingen. After a service of ten years he accepted a similar position at the court of the Margrave of Baden, who acknowledged his abilities by bestowing on him the cross of the order "De la Fidelite."

However, the dignified tranquillity of court life could not satisfy the active and impetous temperament of Steuben for any length of time.

As every former war-horse will listen for the electrifying call of the trumpet, so in the heart of this born soldier the longing for active military service would never die. And he followed the bugle call when, in 1777, while traveling in France, he met again with an old friend, Count St. Germain. This gentleman had been formerly in the service of the King of Denmark. At the close of the Seven Years' War he had met von Steuben quite often and in frequent conversations had formed a high opinion of his military abilities and sound judgment. Now St. Germain was in the service of the King of France, who had appointed him Secretary of War.

Just at that time the political horizon was charged again with electricity. France, during the Seven Years' War, had been robbed by England of all her colonies in Asia as well as in North America, the results of several hundred years of discovery and conquest as well as of an enormous outlay of money. In America France lost her great empires Canada and New France, comprising the wonderful systems of the St. Lawrence as well as of the Ohio and the Mississippi, the best and most fertile parts of the whole continent. In the West Indies France had to surrender the beautiful islands Granada, St. Vincent, Dominique and Tobago, England's magnanimity left to her vanquished neighbor nothing but four insignificant islets in the West Indies and the bare rocks of St. Pierre and Miquelon, south of New Foundland, in the neighborhood of which the French sailors were allowed to fish, so that they might supply their co-religionists with cod fish, the proper food during the holydays. As in our times about Alsace-Lorrain, so France after the humiliating treaty of 1763 was burning with the thirst for revenge. But not strong enough to risk singly another war with England, she was waiting for a chance to retaliate.

The uprising of the British colonies, in North America against the motherland promised all kinds of possibilities. If these rebellious colonies were secretly assisted in their efforts to break their fetters it might mean the beginning of the downfall of the whole British Empire.

It did not take long for the Americans to become aware of this sentiment of the French Government. Accordingly the Continental Congress soon after the Declaration of Independence appointed a commission to go to France and ask her assistance. This committee, consisting of Silas Deane, Arthur Lee and Benjamin Franklin, had orders to solicit money and military supplies as well as to secure, if possible the service of such expert European officers as might be useful to the American cause. Just this question was of eminent importance.

Soon after the outbreak of hostilities the colonists became aware, that their volunteers and militia men were no match for the well trained British soldiers. To be sure, there were a few able Indian fighters, but the majority of the volunteers had not the slightest idea of regular warfare.

In a historical review of the American Army these

men are described as deficient in discipline, in instruction, in equipment, in arms and ammunition, in every military essential—as was inevitable in view of the manner in which they had been brought together. They were enlisted to serve for short periods, for six or nine months, or until the end of the year only. Their company officers were elected by the men, the field officers by the company officers, and the general officers were appointed by Congress. The essential thing was to raise men, and whoever could get together fifty men became a captain; he who could raise 500 men a colonel, regardless of qualifications for command. A few of the officers and men had served in the French and Indian wars, but the number of these was small, and outside of them military training and experience did not exist.

Because of these facts this army had been defeated by the well organized British soldiers in all open battles. But as decisive results could be gained in such engagements only, it was an absolute necessity to put the continental army into such condition that it could risk challenging its opponents in the open field. As the Americans had no experts in the science of war, they had to turn to Europe for instruction and guidance.

At that time the army of Frederick the Great was regarded as the most exemplary in existence, as the model for all others. For this reason, Franklin, assisted by St. Germain, who had implicit faith in Steuben's abilities, tried eagerly to secure Steuben's service for the American cause.

To their great joy he did not require much persuasion. The interest of the German people in America and in American affairs was at all times intense. Many thousands of sturdy men and women had emigrated to the New World, in the hope of finding there better living conditions than in war-ridden Europe.

Now the efforts made by the British colonies to free themselves from their tyrannical motherland intensified this interest, as for centuries the Germans had fought for liberty, political as well as religious. German philosophers, poets and newspapers pronounced the uprising of the American Colonies the most important event of the century, full of promise for a great part of humanity.* And Frederick the Great, that farseeing monarch, favored the American colonist not only by refusing transit through Prussian territory to the British mercenaries, but also by recognizing the independence of the colonies in concluding a treaty of commerce with the United States.**

Steuben likewise had followed the struggle of the American colonists for independence with heartfelt sympathy. How strongly their cause appealed to him, appears from the letter,*** in which, after his arrival in America, he offered his service to the Continental Congress, then in session at York, Pennsylvania. As this letter reveals the character of its writer, it may be given here in full:

"Portsmouth, December 6, 1777.
"Honorable Gentlemen:
"The honor of serving a respectable Nation, engaged in the noble enterprize of defending its rights and Liberty, is the only motive that brought me over to this Continent. I ask neither riches nor titles. I am come here from the remotest end of Germany at my own expense, and have given up an honorable and lucrative rank; I have made no condition with your Deputies in France, nor shall I make any with you. My only ambition is to serve you as a Volunteer, to deserve the confidence of your General in Chief, and to follow him in all his operations, as I have done during seven campaigns with the King of Prussia. Two and twenty years past at such a school seem to give me a right of thinking myself in the number of experienced Officers;

---

* "The Influence of the American Revolution Upon German Literature" is the title of an interesting book by J. T. Hatfield and Elfrieda Hochbaum. London & New York, 1902.

*** Prussia and the United States. Frederick the Great's Influence on the American Revolution. Historical sketch by Frederick F. Schrader. New York, 1923.

** The original of this letter is in the "Papers of the Continental Congress," No. 19 V. folio 547.

and if I am Possessor of some talents in the Art of War, they should be much dearer to me, if I could employ them in the service of a Republick, such as I hope soon to see America. I should willingly purchase at my whole Blood's Experience the honor of seeing one Day my Name after those of the defenders of your Liberty. Your gracious acceptance will be sufficient for me, and I ask no other favour than to be received among your Officers. I dare hope you will agree (to) this my Request, and that you will be so good as to send me your Orders to Boston, where I shall expect them, and accordingly take convenient measures.

"I have the honour to be, with respect, honorable gentlemen,

"Your most obedient and very humble servant,

"Steuben."

On the same day Steuben sent the following letter to George Washington, the Commander in Chief of the American Army:

"Sir: The inclosed copy of a letter, the original of which I shall have the honor to present to Your Excellency, will inform you of the motives that brought me over to this land. I shall only add to it that the object of my greatest ambition is to render the country all the service in my power, and to deserve the title of a citizen of America by fighting for the cause of your liberty. If the distinguished ranks in which I have served in Europe should be an obstacle, I had rather serve under Your Excellency as a volunteer than to be an object of discontent to such deserving officers as have already distinguished themselves among you. Such being the sentiments I have always professed, I dare hope that the respectable Congress of the United States of America will accept my services. I could say, moreover, were it not for the fear of offending your modesty, that Your Excellency is the only person under whom, after having served the King of Prussia, I could wish to follow a profession to the study of which I have wholly devoted myself. I intend to go to Boston in a few days, where I shall present my letters to Mr. Hancock, Member of Congress, and there I shall await Your Excellency's orders."

At Boston, where Steuben was entertained by John Hancock, the former President of the Continental Congress, he awaited the answer to his letters. As communication in those days was slow and irregular, it took weeks before a reply could be expected.
Meanwhile Steuben had ample time to study the situation. As matters were standing, it was the most gloomy period in the entire war. Philadelphia, the colonial capital had been taken by the British, also the fortifications and all American vessels on the Delaware river had been destroyed. The adherents and supporters of the British government at Philadelphia, the Tories, had welcomed General Howe, the British commander-in-chief, with open arms as their deliverer, while the farmers of the surrounding country were only too glad to accept the good British money for their butter, eggs, vegetables and cattle. While the British army was in good condition, awaiting re-enforcements from England, Washington's original force of 17,000 men, after having been defeated at Brandywine and Germantown, had dwindled down to 5012 discouraged men. This so called "Continental Army" was in direst distress, as the Board of War had failed so completely to provide it with supplies, that Washington wrote to Congress: "Unless some great and capital change takes place, the army must inevitably be reduced to one or other of these three things —to starve, dissolve or disperse in order to obtain subsistence."
Besides, the whole country was suffering under a dreadful scarcity of money. To increase these difficulties, the British had resorted to counterfeiting the paper money issued by Congress. Swamping the country with enormous quantities of fraudulent bills, they succeeded in bringing paper money into such discredit, that everybody had the greatest aversion to accepting it. This brought with it an enormous devaluation. Forty paper dollars were equal to one silver dollar. Fourhundred to six hundred dollars was the price of a pair of boots.

And if a soldier would have a square meal, he was compelled to sacrifice a month's pay.

In consideration of all these conditions, and in possession of the two largest cities in America, New York and Philadelphia, General Howe was confident that the rebellion would soon die out.

Well might Thomas Paine declare: "These are the times that try men's souls!"

All these facts must be recalled in order to appreciate, at its full value Steuben's great sacrifice, when he offered his service to such a precarious cause. No soldier of fortune, out for pecuniary gain or other advantages, could have been induced to face a situation, that seemed to promise nothing but failure and misery.

Steuben, however, firm and resolute, did not shrink from the difficult task before him; but awaited calmly the reply to his letters.

Congress, of course, was only too glad to secure the services of a distinguished soldier, who was actuated by such noble motives. On Wednesday, January 14, 1778, it adopted the following resolution.

"Whereas the Baron Steuben, a lieutenant general in foreign service, has, in a most disinterested and heroic manner, offered his services to these States in the quality of a volunteer:

Resolved, that the president present the thanks of Congress, in behalf of these United States, to the Baron Steuben, for the zeal he has shown for the cause of America, and the disinterested tender he has been pleased to make of his military talents; and inform him, that Congress cheerfully accept of his service as a volunteer in the army of these states, and wish him to repair to General Washington's quarters as soon as convenient."

Washington's answer was in a similar vein. It contained the request that Steuben report at once to Congress at York, since that body had the exclusive right to enter into negotiations with him.

When Steuben arrived at this town, he was received with every mark of distinction the situation permitted.

The day after his arrival he was called upon by a committee to confer with him about the conditions under which he was willing to serve the United States, and to ask whether he had made any stipulations with the American commissioners in France. It made the following report:

"The Baron Steuben, who was a lieutenant general, and aide-de-camp to the King of Prussia, desires no rank, is willing to attend General Washington and be subject to his orders; does not require or desire any command of a particular corps or division, but will serve occasionally as directed by the general; expects to be of use in planning encampments, etc., and promoting the discipline of the army. He heard before he left France of the dissatisfaction of the Americans with the promotion of foreign officers, therefore makes no terms, nor will accept of anything but with general approbation, and particularly that of General Washington."

Congress, through its president, Mr. Laurens, accepted the generous proposition of Steuben and directed him to report to General Washington at Valley Forge, a place about 23 miles northwest of Philadelphia.

STEUBEN'S COAT OF ARMS.

In the Winter Camp at Valley Forge.

Steuben arrived at Valley Forge on December 23rd, welcomed most heartily by Washington, who with his staff came several miles to meet him on the road. Certainly it was a moment of extraordinary significance when these two men, who had never seen each other before, shook hands. Both were in the prime of life, Washington not yet 45, Steuben only one and a half years his senior. Both were of splendid figure and dignified demeanor, and both were enthusiastic for the same great cause. According to the descriptions of contemporaries and the portrait from life painted by Ralph Earle, Steuben represented the finest type of the soldiery of Frederick the Great. His countenance displayed a combination of energy and benevolence. His head was round, the forehead large, the nose fine, almost acquiline, while a pair of piercing hazel eyes gave animation to his face, the upper part of which was remarkably expressive of the strong traits of his character.

Bishop Ashbel Greene, who met Steuben somewhat later, has given the following vivid description of Steuben: "Never before or since have I had such an impression of the ancient fabled god of war as when I looked at the Baron; he seemed to me a perfect personification of Mars. The trappings of his horse, the enormous bolsters of his pistols, his large size, and his strikingly martial aspect, all seemed to favor the idea."

When the cavalcade arrived at the camp, Steuben found that Washington had everything prepared in his honor. A note in Steuben's papers says: "Upon my arrival I was again the object of more honors than I was entitled to. The commander-in-chief accompanied me to my quarters, where I found an officer with twenty-five men as a guard of honor. When I declined this, saying that I wished to be considered merely as a vol-

George Washington Commander in Chief of the Army of the American Revolution

From a painting by John Trumbull, now in the City Hall, New York

unteer, the general answered me in the politest words that the whole army would be gratified to stand sentinel for such volunteers. On the same day my name was given as watchword."

That Steuben had made a most favorable impression on the commander-in-chief, appears in the letter by which he notified Congress of Steuben's arrival: "He appears to be much of a gentleman, and so far as I have had an opportunity of judging, a man of military knowledge, and acquainted with the world."

The conditions Steuben was to face at Valley Forge were desparate beyond belief. Such an army of hungry and ragged men he had never seen before. They were living in tents and huts, destitute and in want of practically everything. Suffering from the frost and snow, they were almost without clothing, food, arms and ammunition. Large numbers of the men had no blankets with which to protect themselves against the cold and so they were compelled to sit up all night by the camp-fires for warmth.

The window openings of the log huts were closed with oiled paper, and the cracks between the logs were chinked with wetted clay. As the huts were arranged in parallel streets, each brigade of troops by itself, the whole encampment was similar like those constructed during the 19th century by miners and railroad men in the Far West.

A report of December 23rd stated that "there was not a single hoof of any kind to slaughter, and not more than twenty-five barrels of flour. 2898 men were unfit for duty, because they were barefoot, or otherwise naked."

In a still existing letter Steuben has tried to give his impressions after his arrival: "My determination must have been very firm that I did not abandon my design when I saw these troops. Matters had to be remedied, but where to commence was the great difficulty."

Volumes 11 and 12 of the "Steuben Papers" in the archives of the New York Historical Society contain graphic descriptions of the discouraging disorder that was prevalent. In regard to the army they say:

"I found that the different branches of the army were divided into departments. There were those of the quartermaster-general, war commissary, provisions commissary, commissary of the treasury, or paymaster of forage, etc. etc. But they were all bad copies of a bad original. That is to say, they had imitated the English administration, which is certainly the most imperfect in Europe.

"The effective strength of the Army was divided into divisions, commanded by major generals; into brigades, commanded by brigadier generals; and into regiments, commanded by colonels. The number of men in a regiment was fixed by Congress, as well as in a company—so many infantry, cavalry and artillery. But the eternal ebb and flow of men engaged for three, six, and nine months, who went and came every day, rendered it impossible to have either a regiment or a company complete; and the words company, regiment, brigade, and division were so vague that they did not convey any idea upon which to form a calculation, either of a particular corps or of the Army in general. They were so unequal in their number that it would have been impossible to execute any maneuvers. Sometimes a regiment was stronger than a brigade. I have seen a regiment consisting of thirty men and a company of one corporal. Nothing was so difficult, and often so impossible, as to get a correct list of the state or a return of any company, regiment or corps. As in the English service, there was a muster master general, with a number of assistants. It was the duty of this officer to ascertain and report every month the effective state of the Army, for the payment of the men and officers. This operation took place as follows: Each captain made a roll of his company, whether absent or present, after which he made oath before a superior officer that this return was correct, 'to the best of his knowledge and belief.' The muster master counted the men present, and the absent were marked by him for their pay upon the oath of the captain. I am very far from supposing that an officer would voluntarily commit a fraud, but let us examine the state of the companies, and we shall see the correctness of such returns.

"One company had 12 men present; absent, 1 man as valet to the commissary, 200 miles distant from the army for eighteen months; 1 man, valet to a quartermaster attached to the army of the north, for twelve months; 4 in different hospitals for so many months; 2 as drivers of carriages; and so many more as bakers, blacksmiths, carpenters, even as coal porters, for years together, although the greater number were only engaged for nine months at the outset. But a man once on the roll of a company remained there everlastingly as forming part of the effective strength, except in case of death or desertion under the very eyes of the captain.

"According to these rolls the strength of the Army for pay and provisions was calculated. The regimental returns furnished to the adjutant-general every week, for the information of the general in chief, as to the strength of the Army, were not much more exact. I am sure that at that time a general would have thought himself lucky to find a third of the men ready for action whom he found on paper.

"The soldiers were scattered about in every direction. The Army was looked upon as a nursery for servants, and everyone deemed it his right to have a valet. Several thousand soldiers were employed in this way. We had more commissaries and quartermasters at that time than all the armies of Europe together. The most modest had only one servant, but others had two and even three. If the captains and colonels could give no account of their men, they could give still less an account of their arms, accoutrements, clothing, ammunition, camp equipage, etc. Nobody kept an account but the commissaries, who furnished all the articles. A company which consisted, in May, of 50 men, was armed, clothed, and equipped in June. It then consisted of 30 men. In July it received 30 recruits, who were to be clothed, armed, and equipped; and not only the clothes but the arms were carried off by those who had completed their time of service.

"Gen. Knox assured me that previous to the establishment of my department there never was a campaign in which the military magazines did not furnish from 5,000 to 8,000 muskets to replace those which were lost in the way I have described above.* The loss of bayonets was still greater. The American soldier, never having used this arm, had no faith in it, and never used it but to roast his beefsteak and, indeed, often left it at home. This is not astonishing when it is considered that the majority of the States engaged their soldiers for from six to nine months. Each man who went away took his musket with him, and his successor received another from the public store. No captain kept a book. Accounts were never furnished nor required. As our Army is, thank God, little subject to desertion, I venture to say that during an entire campaign there have not been 20 muskets lost since my system came into force. It was the same with the pouches and other accoutrements, and I do not believe that I exaggerate when I state that my arrangements have saved the United States at least 800,000 French livres a year.

"The arms at Valley Forge were in a horrible condition, covered with rust, half of them without bayonets, many from which a single shot could not be fired. The pouches were quite as bad as the arms. A great many of the men had tin boxes instead of pouches, others had cow horns; and muskets, carbines, fowling pieces, and rifles were to be seen in the same company.

"The description of dress is most easily given. The men were literally naked, some of them in the fullest extent of the word. The officers who had coats had them of every color and make. I saw officers at a grande parade at Valley Forge mounting guard in a sort of dressing gown made of an old blanket or woolen bed cover.** With regard to their military discipline I can safely say no such thing existed. In the first place

---

* The prize of a musket was fixed on the regulations of 1779 at 16 dollars without bayonet, and 18 dollars with bayonet.

** Duponceau, Steuben's secretary and interpreter, has also given a description of the pitiful situation at Valley Forge. He says:
"We were in want of everything. I remember seeing the soldiers

there was no regular formation. A so-called regiment was formed of three platoons, another of five, eight and nine, and the Canadian regiment of twenty-one. The formation of the regiments was as varied as their mode of drill, which only consisted of the manual exercise. Each colonel had a system of his own, the one according to the English, the other according to the Prussian or French style. There was only one thing in which they were uniform, and that was the way of marching in the maneuvers and on the line of march. They all adopted the mode of marching in files used by the Indians.

"It is also necessary to remark that the changing of men, the reductions, and continual incorporations deprived the corps and regiments of all consistence. There was another evil still more subversive of order in an army—the captains and colonels did not consider their companies and regiments as corps confided to them by the United States for the care of the men as well as the preservation of order and discipline. The greater part of the captains had no roll of their companies, and had no idea how many men they had under their orders. When I asked a colonel the strength of his regiment, the usual reply was, 'Something between two and three hundred men.' The colonels, and often the captains, granted leave of absence as they thought proper, and not only that, but permissions to retire from the

popping their heads out of their miserable huts, and calling out in an undertone 'No bread, no soldier!' Their condition was truly pitiful, but their courage and perseverance beyond all praise. We, too, put the best face we could upon the matter. Once, with the Baron's permission, his aides invited a number of young officers to dine at our quarters, on condition that none should be admitted that had on a whole pair of breeches. This was, of course, understood as pars pro toto, but torn clothes were an indispensable requisite for admission, and in this the guests were sure not to fail. The dinner took place. The guests clubbed their rations and we feasted sumptuously on tough beefsteaks and potatoes, with hickory nuts for our desert. Instead of wine we had some kind of spirits, with which we made "salamanders,' that is to say, after filling our glasses, we set the liquor on fire and drank it up, flames and all. Such a set of ragged and at the same time merry fellows were never brought together. The Baron loved to speak of that dinner, and of his 'sans culottes,' as he called us. Thus this denomination was first invented in America, and applied to brave officers and soldiers of our Revolutionary army."

service. The officers were not accustomed to remain with the troops when the Army was in camp; they lived in houses, often several miles distant. In winter quarters they nearly all went home, and there were often not more than four officers with a regiment. I found one regiment commanded by a lieutenant. The idea they had of their duty was that the officers had only to mount guard and put themselves at the head of their regiment or company when they were going into action.

"The internal administration of a regiment and a company was a thing completely unknown. The quartermaster received arms, ammunition, and camp equipage for an entire brigade. The clothing and provisions were distributed in the same way, by brigades. A captain who did not know the number of men in his company could not know the number of the rations and other articles necessary for it. There were absolutely no regulations for the service of the camp and of the guards. Each colonel encamped his regiment according to his fancy. There were guards and pickets, and sometimes too many; but the officers did not know their duty, and in many instances did not understand the object of the guard. An infinity of internal guards for the commissaries of forage and provisions and for the quartermaster weakened the strength of the Army, the more so because these guards were never relieved and remained from one year to another. Their arms were lost, and they were all the servants of the commissary, who often granted them leave not only for six months, but without limitation. It would be an endless task to enumerate the abuses which nearly ruined the Army."

The necessity of internal administration of an army was absolutely unknown to the Americans. From the British they had adopted the custom, that each company and quartermaster had a commission of so many per cent on all money expended. It was natural, therefore, that expense was not spared, that the quartermasters, to increase their income, ordered many articles for which there was no need. And as no one kept records or accounts, except the commissioners who provided the army with the different articles and made bills to suit themselves, graft and dishonesty prevailed everywhere. The terrible drain on public money was increased, as every soldier was permitted to take, at the end of his nine months' service, his entire outfit, weapons included, with him.

Steuben
Maj: Gen

Organizing the Revolutionary Army.

Well aware of these dreadful conditions and the bitter need of reform, Washington requested Steuben to make plans for the establishment of a strict inspection, so that system and uniformity might be introduced into all these matters. Steuben went to work at once and sketched a variety of different plans.

"But" so he states in his letters," it was exceedingly difficult to find an arrangement likely to succeed so as not to disgust the officers belonging to so many different States and to form a plan in conformity with the spirit of the Nation, and with the prejudices, however well or ill founded they might be, against foreigners. I was often obliged to abandon ideas I had formed, also I was in want of information and advice; but I was fortunate enough to find a few officers of merit, who gave me every satisfaction. They were Gen. Greene, Col. Laurens, and Col. Hamilton.

"Having drawn out my last plan, I communicated it to these three officers and made the alterations they deemed advisable before I presented it to the commander-in-chief. Time was precious, therefore I worked day and night. I finally proposed that an inspector general ought to be appointed at once, who should establish a uniform system for forming the troops, for exercising and maneuvering them, for their duties in camp and on the march, and for the duties of guards, pickets and sentries. He should also define and point out the duties of every officer, from the colonel to the corporal; the manner in which returns or lists of the men, arms, accoutrements, clothing, and camp equipage should be made, and appoint a uniform method of bookkeeping, according to which the books of the regiments, of companies, as well as those of the adjutant, paymaster, quartermaster, and clothing master of each regiment should be kept; that the inspector should review

Relief on the Steuben Monument at Valley Forge.
Modeled by J. Otto Schweizer.

the troops every month, exercise and maneuver them, examine the returns and books, and make his written return to the commander-in-chief and to the board of war, etc., that a colonel from each division should be chosen by the inspector general, whose duty it shall be to see that the ordinances and arrangements which the inspector might think proper to establish, with the consent of the commander-in-chief, be duly executed and obeyed."

Enjoying the hearty approval of Washington Steuben began immediately the difficult task of making soldiers out of the recruits. How he did it, is illustrated best by his own story:

"I commenced operations by drafting 120 men from the line, whom I formed into a guard for the general-in-chief. I made this guard my military school. I drilled them myself twice a day, and to remove that English prejudice which some officers entertained, namely, that to drill a recruit was a sergeant's duty and beneath the station of an officer, I often took the musket myself to show the men the manual exercise which I wished to introduce. All my inspectors were present at each drill. We marched together, wheeled, etc., and in a fortnight my company knew perfectly how to bear arms, had a military air, knew how to march, to form in columns, deploy and execute some little maneuvers with excellent precision."

"It must be owned that they did not know much of the manual exercise, and I ought to mention the reasons why I departed altogether from the general rule of all European armies, and commenced with the manual exercise in drilling recruits like children learning their alphabet. In the first place I had no time to do otherwise. In our European armies a man who has been drilled for three months is called a recruit, here in two months I must have a soldier. In Europe we had a number of evolutions very pretty to look at when well executed, but in my opinion absolutely useless so far as essential subjects are concerned. I nevertheless taught my company to carry arms, stand at ease, present arms, to load, take aim, fire by platoons, and to charge bayonets. Another reason that induced me to pay but little attention to this eternal manual exercise was that several of my predecessors commenced with it, and before they had surmounted these preliminaries, were obliged to quit the service, having lost their influence and before the officers had an opportunity of seeing the practical advantage of this elementary instruction. This induced me to revise the old system, and instead of commencing with the manual and platoon exercises and ending with maneuvers, I commenced with maneuvers and ended with the exercises.

"I had my company of guards exactly as I wished them to be. They were well dressed, their arms cleaned and in good order, and their general appearance quite respectable. I paraded them in the presence of all the officers of the army and gave them the opportunity of exhibiting all they knew. They formed in column, deployed, attacked with the bayonet, charged front, etc. It afforded a new and agreeable sight for the young officers and soldiers. Having gained my point, I dispersed my apostles, the inspectors, and my new doctrine was largely embraced. I lost no time in extending my operations on a large scale. I applied my system to battalions, afterwards to brigades and in less than three weeks I executed maneuvers with an entire division in presence of the commander-in-chief."

While to the troops these exercises were a source of astonishment and wonder it cannot be said that all the officers readily submitted to the orders of the foreigner. Some even regarded his work as an unwarranted interference with their own authority and threatened to quit. Referring to this state of affairs Steuben afterwards wrote:

"All the brigadier generals threatened to quit service. I, however, in no way changed my conduct; I continually pursued the object I had in view, and flattered nobody, not even the general-in-chief. The nature of my office in the army obliged me to a severity to which our officers were then little accustomed, but I was equally severe towards my inferiors, and am so still at present. And here is my greatest triumph. The same brigadiers who opposed the inspectorship, are eager today to serve under my orders. The same officers whom I never had flattered honor me now with the title of friend and father. In the military career the testimony of the inferiors is the most honorable; our subalterns used to be our most severe judges. The affection and estimation of my officers fill my heart with the greatest pride and satisfaction."

As in time the officers grasped the importance of the exercises, they also became aware, that their former defeats were due to their inability to sustain a contest against the well organized British soldiers.

A remakable change became manifest also in the general appearance of the troops. The former disregard and neglect gave way to a generous rivalry among the various companies, battalions and regiments, to make the best display in outfit as well as in efficiency.

It is most interesting to hear the comments of two officers, who witnessed Steuben's efforts. There still exists the following letter, dated April 8, 1778, at Valley Forge, written by General A. Scammel to his friend General John Sullivan:

"Baron Steuben sets us a truly noble example. He has undertaken the discipline of the Army, and shows himself to be a perfect master of it, not only in the grand maneuvers, but in the most minute details. To see a gentleman dignified with a lieutenant general's commission from the great Prussian monarch condescend with a grace peculiar to himself to take under his direction a squad of 10 to 12 men in the capacity of drill sergeant, commands the admiration of both officers and men and causes them to improve exceedingly fast under his instructions."

William North,[*] who later on became Steuben's aide-de-camp, made the following comments:

---

[*] Wm. North, born in 1755 at Fort Frederick, Maine, entered the Revolutionary army when he was twenty. In 1779 he was appointed aide-de-camp to General Steuben and served on his staff until the end of the war. Some time before his death, which happened in January, 1836 at New York, North wrote a short sketch of Baron Steuben's life. These notes were later on published by one of North's descendants in the Magazine of American History of March, 1882.

"Certainly it was a brave attempt. Without understanding a word of the English language, to think of bringing men, born free and joined together to preserve their freedom, into strict subjection, to obey without a word, a look, the mandates of a master—that master once their equal, or, possibly, beneath them.... It was a brave attempt which nothing but virtue or high-raised hopes of glory could have supported.

"From the commencement of instruction no time, no pains, no fatigue were thought too great in pursuit of this great object. Through the whole of each campaign when troops were to maneuver, and that almost every day, the baron rose at 3 o'clock. While his servant dressed his hair, he smoked a single pipe and drank one coup of coffee; was on horseback at sunrise, and, with or without his suite, galloped to the parade. There was no waiting for a tardy aide-de-camp, and those who followed wished they had not slept. Nor was there need of chiding; when duty was neglected or military etiquette infringed, the baron's look was enough."

As is stated in the above comment, Steuben's success was astonishing even the more, as at that time his knowledge of English was almost nil. But his occasional bad breaks in this language did not at all cause disrespect, but amusement; especially, when he, in despair about the slowness of some soldiers to grasp the meaning of a command, began to swear and, in a droll mixture of three languages asked his aide-de-camp to swear for him in English. "Viens, mon ami Walker, viens mon bon ami. Sacra—g—dam de gaucheries of these badauds, je ne puis plus—I can curse them no more! Die Dummköpfe will not do what I bide them!" But while the soldiers chuckled over such funny incidents, they all tried their best to obey the orders in a conscious manner.

In that way Steuben infused the whole army with a sense of discipline and order. Giving confidence to the officers and men, and enabling the troops from different parts of the country to act together with unanimity and effect, he rapidly converted the army into an efficient fighting machine.

To regulate the imperfect construction of the army, Steuben submitted a proposition, which on May 27, was adopted by Congress in the following resolution:

THE INFANTRY.

"Resolved, that each battalion of infantry shall consist of nine companies, one of which shall be of light infantry; the light infantry to be kept complete by drafts from the battalion, and organized during the campaign into corps of light infantry. That the battalion of infantry shall consist of:

1 Colonel	27 Sergeants.
1 Lieutenant-Colonel	1 Drum-major.
1 Major.	1 Fife-major.
6 Captains.	18 Drums and Fifes.
1 Captain-Lieutenant.	27 Corporals.
8 Lieutenants	477 Privates.
9 Ensigns.	1 Paymaster to be taken
1 Surgeon.	from the line.
1 Surgeon's Mate.	1 Adjutant, as above.
1 Sergeant-major.	1 Quartermaster, as
1 Quartermaster's Serg.	above.

THE ARTILLERY.

That a battalion of artillery shall consist of:

1 Colonel.	1 Fife-Major.
1 Lieutenant-Colonel.	72 Sergeants.
1 Major.	72 Bombardiers.
12 Captains.	72 Corporals.
12 Captain-Lieutenants.	72 Gunners.
12 First Lieutenants.	24 Drums and Fifes
36 Second Lieutenants.	336 Matrosses.
1 Surgeon.	1 Paymaster, to be taken
1 Surgeon's Mate.	from the line.
1 Sergeant-Major.	1 Adjutant, as above.
1 Quartermaster's Serg.	1 Quartermaster as
1 Drum-Major.	above.

THE CAVALRY, OR DRAGOONS.

That a battalion of cavalry shall consist of

1 Colonel.	6 Captains.
1 Lieutenant-Colonel.	6 Quartermaster's Serg.
1 Major.	6 Trumpeters.

12 Sergeants.
374 Dragoons.
12 Lieutenants.
6 Cornets.
1 Surgeon.
1 Surgeon's Mate.
1 Saddler.
1 Trumpet-Major

6 Farriers.
1 Paymaster to be taken from the line.
1 Adjutant, as above.
1 Quartermaster, as above.
30 Corporals.

PROVOSTS.

That a provost be established to consist of:

1 Captain of Provosts.
4 Lieutenants.
1 Clerk.
1 Quartermaster's Sergt.
2 Trumpeters.

2 Sergeants.
3 Corporals.
43 Provosts or Privates.
4 Executioners.

In the Engineering Department three companies be established, each to consist of:

1 Captain.
3 Lieutenants.
4 Sergeants.

4 Corporals.
60 Privates.

That two aides-de-camp be allowed to each major-general, who shall for the future appoint them out of the captains and subalterns."

We hardly need to mention that Steuben also made great efforts to secure regular uniforms for his troops. But this was an embarrassing task, as the poverty of the country and the difficulty of procuring supplies from abroad were such that it was not till 1782 that the army was completely uniformed and armed. A general order, issued from headquarters at New Windsor, N. Y., October 2, 1779, directed that the regiments of New Hampshire, Massachusetts, Rhode Island and Connecticut should be uniformed in blue, faced with white; those of New York and New Jersey in blue, faced with buff; of Pennsylvania, Delaware, Maryland and Virginia, in blue, faced with red; of North Carolina, South Carolina and Georgia, in blue, faced with blue. The light dragoons were to wear blue faced with white, and the colors of the artillery were to be blue and red.

The various grades of the officers were distinguished

Uniforms of the American Army, 1779-1784

	Major General.	Aide de Camp.	Line Officer.
Colors:	Blue faced with buff	Blue faced with buff.	Blue faced with red.

From Plate III of "Uniforms of the Army of the United States" published by the Quartermaster General.

by ribbons of different colors worn across the breast, and by various cockades and feathers on their hats. But among the provincial troops and their officers an endless variety of clothing and equipment prevailed throughout the revolution.

While Steuben so successfully improved all conditions of the army he also tried to correct the many evils that under the administration of Thomas Conway, an Irishman, had taken root in all departments, especially in those, that had to do with furnishing the troops with the necessaries of life and military equipment. Graft and dishonesty prevailed everywhere, causing those terrible sufferings which in the winter encampment at Valley Forge had reached their climax. Washington, greatly disturbed about these conditions requested Steuben to submit propositions for reforms.

"The general" so Steuben says in his notes, "asked me to give him some statements concerning the arrangements of the departments and their various branches in the European armies. I gave them to him, and detailing therein the duties of each department and of its different branches, dilated upon the functions of the quartermasters in particular, in which branch I had served myself for a long time in the Seven Year's War. But the English system, bad as it is, had already taken root. Each company and quartermaster had a commission of so much per cent on all money expended. It was natural, therefore, that expense was not spared—that wants were discovered where there were none; and that the dearest articles were those that suited the commissioners the best. Hence the depreciation of our currency; hence the expense of so many millions.

"I pointed out to General Washington and several members of Congress the advantages of the contract system. I even drew up a memorandum on the subject, which Colonel Laurens translated into English, showing the way in which things were contracted for in Prussian and French armies. But whether it was that they thought such a system impracticable in this country, or whether they were unable to check the torrent of expense, things remained as they were."

That Steuben's efforts in this direction had little effect, can not surprise us when we consider the make-up of the so-called Continental Congress. This body had come in existence, when, following a call of Massachusetts in September 1774, fifty-three colonial delegates had assembled at Philadelphia, where they drew the famous address to the King and the address to the People of Great Britain. This Congress was followed by another in May 1775. It acted under no constitutional authority whatever. As set forth in an article by Bach McMaster in Harpers Monthly of April, 1889: "The States were parties to no instrument of government, and every act committed by their delegates was done with the tacit or express consent of the States. No system of representation was in use. To the secret deliberations of the little body that bore the name of the Congress came delegates chosen in such a way and in such numbers and bearing such instructions as best pleased the States that sent them. Once seated in Congress, these men found themselves members of what a few years later would have been denounced as a "dark and secret conclave." The doors were shut, no spectators were suffered to hear what was said; no reports of the debates were taken in short-hand or long-hand; but under a strict injunction of secrecy they went on deliberating day after day. From month to month so much of the journal as Congress thought fit was indeed given to the people; but Congress thought fit to give merely a dry record of ordinances passed, or motions made, of reports read, of committees chosen. Over these deliberations presided a President elected by the Congress, and looked up to as the representative of the sovereignty of the States united for common defence. As such, his house, his table, his servants, were all provided at public cost. But the expense of every other delegate was borne by the State that sent him.

"Thus formed, the Continental Congress proceeded without any authority, to raise armies, equip navies, to borrow money, to send out ministers, to make treaties, and do innumerable acts of sovereignty in the name of the States. It was Congress that commissioned Washington; that sent Franklin to the court of France; that voted the Declaration of Independence; that framed the Articles of Confederation; that advised the Colonies, in the quaint language of the resolution "to take up civil government."

"Most of the Congress' dealings was with the States. In but a few ways did it touch the people, and in the most delicate of these its record is that of disaster after disaster. The bills of credit which no one would take, the loan offices set up in every State, the Congress lottery that failed so miserably, commissary certificates, interest incidents, were constant reminders of the financial imbecility of Congress, and did far more to bring it into contempt than any of its great acts did to bring it into honor."

While under such conditions Steuben's efforts to remedy the evils, must fail, his full success in regard of the organization of the army impressed the commander-in-chief so deeply, that he on the 30th of April, 1778, ten weeks after Steuben had commenced his active duties, made the following report to Congress:

"The extensive ill consequences arising from a want of uniformity in discipline and maneuvers throughout the Army have long occasioned me to wish for the establishment of a well-organized inspectorship, and the concurrence of Congress in the same views has induced me to set on foot a temporary institution, which, from the success which has hitherto attended it, gives me the most flattering expectations, and will, I hope, obtain their approbation.

"Baron de Steuben's length of service in the first military school in Europe, and his former rank, pointed him out as a person peculiarly qualified to be at the head of this department; this appeared the least exceptionable way of introducing him into the army, and one that would give him the most ready opportunity of displaying his talents. I therefore proposed to him to undertake the office of Inspector General, which he agreed to with the greatest cheerfulness, and has performed the duties of it with a zeal and intelligence equal to our wishes.

"I should do injustice, if I were to be longer silent with regards to the merits of the Baron de Steuben. His knowledge of his profession, added to the zeal which he has displayed since he began upon the functions of his office, leads me to consider him an acquisition to the service, and to recommend him to the attention of Congress."

Congress approved on May 5th General Washington's recommendations and appointed Steuben to the office of Inspector General, with the rank and pay of major-general, his pay to commence from the time he had joined the army and entered into the service of the United States.

This resolution arrived at Valley Forge at the same time when intelligence came that a treaty of commerce and alliance had been ratified with France. This great event was celebrated on May 6th with a grand maneuver by the entire army. Directed by von Steuben, and executed by the Generals Stirling, De Kalb and Lafayette, it passed off most successfully. It was followed by a dinner, during which Washington informed Steuben of his commission of Major-General and inspector of the army, and at the next morning Washington issued the following order:

"The commander-in-chief takes great pleasure in acquainting the army that its conduct yesterday afforded him the highest satisfaction. The exactness and order with which all its movements were formed, is a pleasing evidence of the progress it has made in military improvement, and of the perfection to which it may arrive by a continuance of that laudable zeal which now happily prevails. The general, at the same time, presents his thanks to Baron Steuben and the gentlemen acting under him for their exertions in the duties of their office, the good effects of which are already so apparent, and for the care, activity and prosperity with which they conducted the business of yesterday."

The Battle at Monmouth and the Treason of General Lee.

It did not take long for the results of the many improvements, introduced by Steuben, to become evident. This was on June the 28th in the battle at Monmouth, N. J.

During the spring the American forces at Valley Forge had increased from 5,000 to 15,000 men. All these men were well drilled by Steuben, and all were eager to show their efficiency. Such an opportunity came soon enough. The report that France had entered an open alliance with the United States and that a strong fleet was under way to assist the Americans in their struggle for liberty, caused the British to evacuate Philadelphia and concentrate at New York. The army, 17,000 strong, crossed the Delaware on the 18th of June and was on its march through New Jersey. 3000 Tories with their effects were sent to New York around by water. Eager to inflict a heavy blow upon the retreating enemy, Washington set his army on pursuit. Steuben reconnoitring on the morning of June 27th, had made out the position of the British troops, whereupon Washington ordered General Charles Lee to attack the enemy's rear with his advance guard. At the same time the main body was put in motion. The right wing of the army was commanded by General Greene, and the left wing by Lord Stirling. Washington was with the left wing, with Steuben attached to his staff.

But the confidence Washington had placed in Lee, was not at all justified, as this man was the real type of an unscrupulous soldier of fortune, ever ready to sell out as soon as an opportunity would arrive and a goodly price be offered. Born in 1731 in England, he had fought as a British officer in America against the French and the Indians, with Portuguese troops against the Spaniards, and with Russian Cossacks against the

Turks. In 1773 he came to America again, where he took up the cause of the colonists, to get even with the British government, by whom for certain reasons he felt offended.

As his many adventures gave him a certain prestige, he was welcomed as a valuable acquisition by Washington. Congress even made him major general, in which rank, after the resignation of General Ward, he became the senior officer, with prospects that by the death or displacement of Washington he would become the commander-in-chief.

That Lee secretly aspired to this post, is proven by several letters, by which he tried to stir disaffection in order to undermine Washington's position. In a confidential letter addressed to General Gates, he came out with the remark that "a certain great man is most damnably deficient." Other letters contain hints of very important things he could perform, if he were made dictator. More than once he disregarded orders coming from the commander-in-chief, thus endangering the success of momentous movements.

Through his own carelessness Lee was captured in December, 1776, by the British dragoons and taken to New York. Sir William Howe, the British Commander, intended to hang him as a deserter, having been an officer in the British army; but unfortunately he concluded to report to his government in London and ask for instructions. Orders came to send the prisoner to England for trial. Washington, hearing of these proceedings asked for Lee's release, threatening that five British officers, captured by the Americans, would be held as hostages for Lee's safety. An exchange was made on April 21, 1778, and it was in May, when Lee arrived at Valley Forge.

But he was no longer a fighter for the American cause, but a mean, cold blooded traitor.

While confined in New York, he had made up his mind to betray his former comrades in arms. For the purpose of winning the favor of Sir William Howe and of saving his own life, he had drawn up a plan of operation against the Americans. In this paper Lee declared that the people of Maryland and Pennsylvania were "loyal," with exception of "the populous German districts Frederic County in Maryland and York in Pennsylvania." In speaking of these Germans he says: "They are extremely numerous, and to a man have hitherto been the most staunch assertors of the American cause." To subdue these colonists and to dictate terms to the Americans, Lee suggested a plan of campaign by which the British might capture Philadelphia, Annapolis and Alexandria and drive Washington out of New Jersey. While 14,000 men should perform the latter part of the program, 4,000 men should sail for the Chesapeake bay, to take the above named cities.

If Howe had been in a position to carry out Lee's plan immediately, Philadelphia would have fallen several months earlier instead of in September, 1777. Also the capture of Burgoyne's army at Saratoga might have been prevented and thus the full success of the British arms might have been assured.

When Lee arrived at Valley Forge, Washington and his generals of course were unaware of his treason as well as of the fact that he had accepted from Howe 1100 guineas for further services. And so Lee was replaced in the same position he had held before.

At Monmouth Lee by seniority had been placed in command of the entire advance. But with treason in his heart, he resorted to the foulest tricks to prevent the breaking up of the retreating British army. First, he executed Washington's orders in a manner so slow and unsatisfactory, that the British had ample time to prepare not only for resistance but for a resolute attack.

Furthermore Lee, by embarrassing his officers with orders and counter-orders, caused such confusion amongst his own regiments that they were compelled to fall back to escape annihilation.

A complete rout seemed imminent. Informed of the threatening situation by estafettes sent by some of Lee's officers, Washington speeded with his staff to the point of danger. Savage with anger, he rebuked Lee furiously and sent him back to the rear. Then taking the command, he ordered Steuben to rally the fleeing troops behind the line of battle and turn them back again.

It was the first time that the American troops had, in face of an advancing enemy, to perform such a difficult problem. But under Steuben's able direction they executed this feat so rapidly and with such precision as they could not have done better during a parade. In very short time Steuben was able to march three brigades into the firing line. After another hour the British were repulsed. Washington then taking the offensive, remained master of the field, camping with his army on the grounds, and ready to renew the attack in the morning. But when the Americans rose there was no one to be attacked, for the British had crept off during the night, leaving all their wounded and dead behind. Having marched away in a hurry, they were too far away to be overtaken.

So Steuben's successful maneuvering had brought victory out of defeat. Colonel Alexander Hamilton, who was an eye witness of the performance, declared that he then for the first time became aware of the overwhelming importance of military training and discipline. The greatest triumph, however, was that Steuben's system of drilling, reviews, inspections, and reports imbued the officers as well as the soldiers with the confidence that from now on they were on equal footing with the armies of the enemy.

The day after the battle General Lee, whose traitorous scheme had failed, directed an impudent letter to Washington, demanding an apology for the rebuke and the brusque language he had used in presence of his officers. As Washington denied such an apology. adding that Lee should have the opportunity of justifying himself to Congress, Lee addressed another letter to the commander-in-chief, which contained the following remarks:

"You cannot afford me greater pleasure than in giving me the opportunity of showing to America the sufficiency of her respective servants. I trust that temporary power of office and the tinsel dignity attending it will not be able, by all the mists they can raise, to obfuscate the bright rays of truth."

The result of this letter was that Lee was placed under arrest and that a court martial was appointed, to investigate his behaviour. It found him guilty of disobedience of orders, of misbehaviour on the battle field in making an unnecessary and shameful retreat, and of disrespect to the commander-in-chief.

Steuben appeared as one of the witnesses at this court martial. This caused Lee to speak of him as "one of all the very distant spectators," a remark that irritated Steuben to such an extent, that he on December 2, directed to Lee the following letter:

"It has been reported to me. sir, that in your defense you have allowed yourself to cast indecent reflections on my account. I made haste to arrive at Philadelphia to inquire into the matter, and I find the report confirmed by the journal of the court martial, of which I got possession an hour ago, and where I read the following paragraph: 'Of all the very distant spectators, etc.' Were I now in my own country where my reputation is long established, I should have put myself above your epigrams and would have despised them. But here I am a stranger. You have offended me, I desire you will give me satisfaction. You will chose the place, time and arms, but as I do not like to be a distant or slow spectator, I desire to see you as near and as soon as possible. You will explain to Captain Walker, who will deliver this to you, if your present situation will permit you to bring this affair to as quick a conclusion as I wish it."

But Lee was not in the mood to risk his precious life in a duel. So he sent the following apology:

"I believe you have misunderstood the sense of this article of my defense. Very likely the sentence 'very distant spectators' has appeared to you a reflection cast upon your courage. If such be your opinion, I assure you that I had not the least idea of it. I am ready to acknowledge it to all the gentlemen of your acquaintance, to all the world if you will. It is true that I found fault with your forwardness (as I took it to be) to witness against me. I was piqued and thought myself justified in making use of the phrase which you have seen in print, but I repeat it without the least intention of intimating a reflection on your courage."

With this apology which was accepted by Steuben, the controversy was ended.

The court martial suspended Lee from any command in the army for a period of twelve months. As towards the termination of his suspension Lee directed an insolent letter to the president of Congress, he was summarily dismissed.

Convincing proofs of Lee's treason were not discovered for many years after his death. They consist in the original of the paper handed by him to Sir William Howe, which was found and purchased in 1857 by Dr. George H. Moore in England, and is now in the archives of the New York Public Library.*

To seduce American officers and troops to treason, was a method of warfare to which the British constantly resorted. Assisted by loyal Tories many attempts were made to capture or murder even the American commander-in-chief. One day evidence was discovered that such treasonable sentiments had taken root even among Washington's bodyguard. So it became necessary to dismiss it and to form a new guard. It consisted almost entirely of Pennsylvania Germans from Berks and Lancaster Counties, who were regarded as the most reliable and trustworthy men among the American troops. This guard, 150 strong, and known as "The Independent Troop of Horse," was commanded by Major Bartholomaeus von Heer, a former cavalry officer in the army of Frederick the Great. Jacob Meytinger served as colonel, and Philipp Struebing and Johann Mutter as lieutenants. The members served also as dispatch bearers, carrying Washington's orders to the various commanders. This guard accompanied Washington throughout the whole war, protecting him faithfully.

---
* A paper on the subject was read by Dr. George H. Moore before the New York Historical Society in June, 1858. In an enlarged form it was published in 1860 as "The Treason of Charles Lee, Major-General, second in command in the American army of the Revolution.

Steuben's "Regulations," the First Manual for the American Army.

The rest of the summer as well as fall 1778 passed by, without other important engagements. Clinton, having reached New York, concentrated his army here and in Newport, while Washington took positions at White Plains, thirty miles north of New York.

Neither party was strong enough to check and overwhelm the other, and so there was a time of "watchful waiting." The French fleet arriving in July made efforts to engage the British fleet in battle, but failing, went to the West Indies, to ravish Jamaica and other British islands.

After the battle at Monmouth Steuben had been appointed temporarily to command the division of General Lee, the traitor. But after arrival of the army at White Plains, this division was placed under Washington's own command, while Steuben was directed to resume his office as inspector general.

It is only natural that Steuben should desire to have an active part in the campaigns also, and thereby win greater fame. He would not be merely the drillmaster of the troops, but wished to command them personally in battle, to demonstrate their ability. Washington, acknowledging the merits of such desire, would have been only too glad, to comply. But it soon became apparent that this was out of the question, at least at the present. There existed among the native born officers a strong current of jealousy and prejudice against all foreign-born officers. Eager to secure the leading positions for themselves they resorted to all sorts of obstructions and intrigues, thus quite often causing the officers of foreign descent to loose their success in military actions.

Such jealousy became evident even after the battle of Monmouth. Complaining that the army during the march from New Jersey to White Plains had been commanded all by foreigners, namely by Steuben, De Kalb and Lafayette, the American born brigadiers objected to have foreigners advanced over their heads. As a number of brigadiers threatened to resign, Washington found himself compelled to make the best of the situation. He therefore tried to induce Steuben to waive his claim to a command. In a letter, directed on July 26 to the President of Congress, he described the situation as follows:

"Justice concurring with inclination constrains me to testify that the Baron has, in every instance, discharged the several trusts reposed in him with great zeal and ability, so as to give him the fullest title to my esteem as a brave, indefatigable, judicious and experienced officer. I regret there should be a necessity that his services should be lost to the army; at the same time I think it my duty explicitly to observe to Congress that his desire of having an actual and permanent command in the line cannot be complied with without wounding the feelings of a number of officers whose rank and merits give them every claim to attention, and that the doing of it would be productive of much dissatisfaction and extensive ill consequences. This does not proceed from any personal objections on the part of those officers against the Baron; on the contrary, most of them whom I heard speak of him, express a high sense of his military worth. It proceeds from motives of another nature, which are too obvious to need particular explanation, or may be summed up in this, that they conceive such a step would be injurious to their essential rights and just expectations. That this would be their way of thinking upon the subject I am fully convinced, from the effect which the tempurary command given him, even under circumstances so peculiar as I have mentioned, produced. The strongest symptoms of discontent appeared on that occasion."

Steuben prompted by his desire to serve the great cause in every respect, yielded to Washington's request and devoted himself again to the manifold duties of inspector-general.

"I shall," so he wrote to the commander-in-chief,

"endeavor to convince Your Excellency and the whole army, that nothing but the good of the service, and not any personal views, shall direct my actions. The American soldier under my orders is, at the same time, a member of the republic I serve. If every officer and soldier would consider me in the same light, it seems to me many obstacles would be avoided. With respect to Your Excellency, I again beg you to consider me as an instrument in your hands for the good of the army which has the honor to serve under your orders."

When winter interrupted military operations, Steuben commenced to prepare a complete book of regulations for the army. It is a manual, which under the title "REGULATIONS FOR THE ORDER AND DISCIPLINE OF THE TROOPS OF THE UNITED STATES" embodies in 25 chapters everything necessary in connection with troops, their weapons, exercises, marching, camping, maneuvering, signal service, inspection, aid and treatment of the sick and wounded. With this invaluable book, known in the army as "Steuben's Regulations" or "The Blue Book," the officers of the American Army received for the first time a clear and definite guide for the performance of their duties.

In composing this manual many difficulties had to be overcome. As it was to be printed in the English language, and as it was essential that every word should be to the point, Steuben secured the assistance of Colonel Fleury, of engineer De L'Enfant, Captain Walker, and of M. Duponceau, his secretary. This fact led Friedrich Kapp to say in his splendid biography of Steuben: "Seldom was a work composed in such a manner as this. Every chapter was first roughly written in German, then translated into bad French, then put in good French by Fleury, translated again into bad English by Duponceau, afterwards written in good English by Captain Walker, and when all this was completed, Steuben did not understand a word of it himself, from his ignorance of the English language."

In quoting this story, Joseph B. Doyle, the American biographer of Steuben felt obliged to say: "Notwithstanding our respect and admiration for Mr. Kapp's careful researches we are inclined to question the accuracy of this statement. Baron Steuben had now been in the country about sixteen months. During that period he was constantly in association with men who spoke only English, was compelled to give orders to troops who knew no other language, and in various ways came in close contact with it almost every hour of the twenty-four, except the limited period alloted to sleep. He was well educated and was already proficient in French as well as his native German. It is not possible that he had learned to speak English fluently during the time he had been in America, in fact he never did so, but it is in the highest degree improbable that in all that time he had not learned to understand a word of this language. The Baron was not able to write out his book in English in the first place, but when translated by his assistants there is no reason to suppose that he was unable to read it, or to understand substantially what it meant."

A perusal of this remarkable book is of great interest not only for military tacticians, but civilians as well. Here is the full list of its contents.

Chapter 1. Of the Arms and Accoutrements of the Officers, Non-Commissioned Officers and Soldiers.

Chapter 2. Objects with which the Officers and Non-Commissioned Officers should be acquainted.

Chapter 3. Of the Formation of a Company.
Chapter 4. Of the Formation of a Regiment.
Chapter 5. Of the Instruction of Recruits.
Chapter 6. The Exercise of a Company.
    Art. 1. Of the opening the Ranks for Inspection.
    Art. 2. Of the Firing.
    Art. 3. Of the March.
    Art. 4. Of the Wheelings.
    Art. 5. Of breaking off and forming by the Oblique Step.

Chapter 7. Exercise of a Battalion.
Chapter 8. Of the Formation and Displaying of Columns, with the Method of Changing Front.
    Art.1. The Close Column formed on the Ground by the Right, the Right in Front.

Art. 2. The Display of a Column formed by the Right, the Right in Front
Art. 3. The close Column formed on the Ground by the Left, the Left in Front.
Art. 4. Display of Column formed by the Left, the Left in Front.
Art. 5. The close Column formed on the Center, or Fifth Platoon, the Right in Front.
Art. 6. Display of a Column having the Right in Front, the Centre or Fifth Platoon.
Art. 7. The close Column formed by the Right, Right in Front, displayed to the Right.
Art. 8. The close Column formed by the Left, Left in Front, displayed to the Left.
Art. 9. Of open Columns.
Art. 10. Of changing the Front of a Line.
Chapter 9. Of the March of Columns.
Art. 1. The march of an open Column.
Art. 2. Columns changing the Directions of their march.
Art. 3. Passage of a Defile by a Column.
Art. 4. A Column crossing a Plain liable to be attacked by Cavalry.
Art. 5. A Column marching by its Flank.
Chapter 10. Of the March in Line.
Art. 1. The March to the Front.
Art. 2. Of the Charge with the Bayonets.
Art. 3. Method of passing any obstacle in Front of a Line.
Art. 4. Passage of a Defile in Front by Platoons.
Art. 5. Passage of a Defile in Front, by Files.
Art. 6. Of the March in Retreat.
Art. 7. Passage of a Defile in Retreat, by Platoons.
Art. 8. Passage of a Defile in Retreat, by Files.
Art. 9. Method of passing the Front Line to the Rear.
Chapter 11. Of the Disposition of the Field-pieces attached to the Brigades.
Chapter 12. Of the Firings.
Art. 1. Firing by Battalion.

Uniforms of the American Army 1779-1784
Artillery

Colors: Blue faced with red.

From plate V of " Uniforms of the Army of the United States."
Published by the Quartermaster General.

Art. 2. Firing by Divisions and Platoons.
Art. 3. Firing advancing.
Art. 4. Firing retreating.
Chapter 13. Of the March of an Army or Corps.
Chapter 14. Of the Baggage on the March.
Chapter 15. The Manner of laying out a Camp, with the Order of Encampment.
Chapter 16. Manner of entering a Camp.
Chapter 17. Necessary Regulations for preserving Order and Cleanliness in the Camp.
Chapter 18. Of Roll-calls.
Chapter 19. Of the Inspection of the Men, their Dress, Necessaries, Arms, Accoutrements and Ammunition.
Chapter 20. Of the different Beats of the Drum.
Chapter 21. Of the Service of the Guards.
    Art. 1. Of the different Guards, with their Use.
    Art. 2. Of the Grand Parade.
    Art. 3. Of relieving Guards and Sentinels.
    Art. 4. Instructions to Officers on Guard.
    Art. 5. Method of going and receiving the Grand Rounds.
    Art. 6. Honors due from Guards to General Officers and others.
Chapter 22. Of the Arms and Ammunition, with the Method of preserving them.
Chapter 23. Of the Treatment of the Sick.
Chapter 24. Of Reviews.
    Art. 1. Of Reviews of Parade.
    Art. 2. Of Reviews of Inspection.
Instructions for the Commandant of a Regiment.
    for the Major
    for the Adjutant
    for the Quarter-Master
    for the Captain
    for the Lieutenant
    for the Ensign
    for the Sergeant-Major
    for the Quarter-Master Sergeant
    for the First Sergeant of a Company

for the Sergeants and Corporals
for the Private Soldier
Chapter 25. Of the Points of View.
Manual Exercise and Evolutions of the Cavalry.

The original scheme included two more divisions: namely of troops in garrison, and of the light infantry. Unfortunately, however, these parts were never printed.

That Steuben in composing this manual, did not merely copy the regulations of the Prussian army, but followed his own ideas, is clearly shown by the fact, that he created an entirely new military organization, the light infantry, unknown before. In Europe armies were always made up of large masses who fought their battles in closed formation and on open fields. But as the eastern parts of North America at these times were covered with thick forests such open fields and wide plains did not exist. Besides, the solitary settlers, in their frequent skirmishes with the Indians, were accustomed to fight singly, independent of others and relying entirely on their own judgment and best abilities.

Taking these facts into careful consideration Steuben instructed the members of the light infantry to fight in a scattered manner, and so they were able to overcome any difficulties of the ground, like hills, rocks, creeks and swamps. This new formation proved such a great success, that from now it became a standing institution in the American army.

To Steuben it was a matter of great satisfaction that his former master Frederick the Great, who studied the American War very closely, introduced the light infantry for his own army.

Steuben's ideas concerning the sanitary conditions of military camps were far advanced for that period. This fact is proven by the seventeenth chapter of the manual, which treats the regulations for presering order and cleanliness in the camps. Indeed it would be difficult for us to-day to improve on these instructions.

Steuben's humanitarian spirit is manifest in the following instructions for the commandant of a regiment:

"The State having entrusted the commandant with the care of a regiment, his greatest ambition should be to have it at all times and in every respect as complete as possible. To do which, he should pay great attention to the following subjects: The preservation of the soldiers' health should be the first and greatest care; and as that depends in a great measure on their cleanliness and manner of living, he must have a watchful eye over the officers of companies, that they pay the necessary attention to their men in those respect."

The instructions for the captains open with the following words:

"A captain cannot be too careful of the company the State has committed to his charge. He must pay the greatest attention to the health of his men, their discipline, arms, accoutrements, ammunition, clothes and necessaries. His first object should be to gain the love of his men by treating them with every possible kindness and humanity, inquiring into their complaints, and, when well founded, seeing them redressed. He should know every man of his company by name and character. He should often visit those who are sick, speak tenderly to them, see that the public provision, whether of medicine or diet, is duly administered, and procure them, besides, such comforts and conveniences as are in his power. The attachment that arises from this kind of attention to the sick and wounded is almost inconceivable; it will, moreover, be the means of preserving the lives of many valuable men."

Congress on March 29, 1779, approved Steuben's work and ordered 3,000 copies to be printed and distributed among the officers of the army. But to have the "Regulations" published, was also a difficult job.

Wm. North, the aide-de-camp of Steuben, says in his notes: "To sketch, re-sketch the plates, and fit them for the engraver—the engraver, the paper, the types and printer, with difficulty to be found. None but those who lived in these dark days of poverty and dearth of everything, can think a thousandth part of all the penury with which we were surrounded. The Blue Book has at last appeared and was studied, and except the Bible, was held in the highest estimation."

In what regard the "Blue Book" was held by the army appeared from the "Creed", adopted by the officers of the American army in 1782 at Verplanck's Point. It reads as follows:

"We believe that there is a great First Cause by whose almighty will we were formed; and that our business here is to obey the orders of our superiors. We believe that every soldier who does his duty will be happy here, and that every such one who dies in battle, will be happy hereafter. We believe that George Washington is the only fit man in the world to head the American army. We believe that Nathaniel Greene was born a general. We believe that the evacuation of Ticonderoga was one of those strokes which stamp the man who dares to strike them, with everlasting fame. We believe that Baron Steuben has made us soldiers, and that he is capable of forming the whole world into a solid column, and displaying it from the center. We believe in his Blue Book. We believe in General Knox and his artillery. And we believe in our bayonets. Amen!"

In what high regard Steuben was held by his soldiers, appears also from a letter by General Howe, who in November, 1782, wrote from his winter camp to Steuben: "Your children, for so I call our army, have been laboring day and night and build their huts. I cannot conclude this letter without conveying to you what I am sure your attachment to the army will render pleasing to you, that they universally think and speak of you with love, pleasure, gratitude and applause."

Editions of the "Regulations" were printed in nearly all the States in 1793 and 1794, to meet the requirements of the Militia act of May 8, 1792. These "Regulations" remained in use for a long time after Steuben's death, until new inventions and new conditions in the mode of warfare made changes necessary.

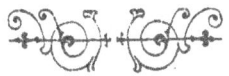

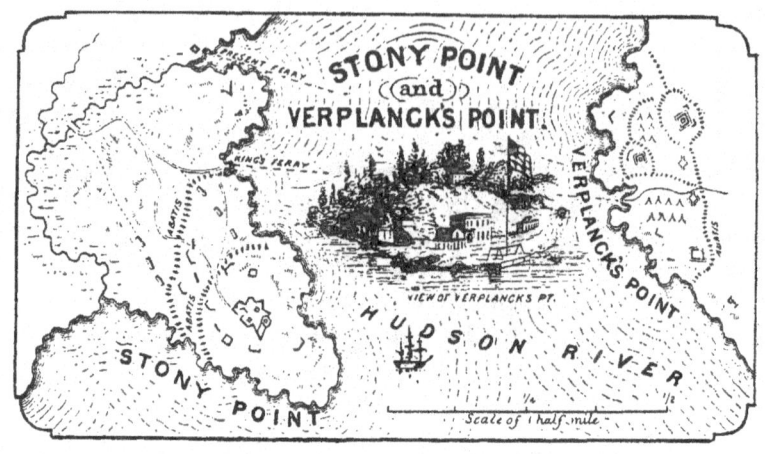

Watchful Waiting in the Highlands of the Hudson.

The military situation during spring 1779 remained practically the same as it had been in fall. The British army, numbering 17,000 men, was still concentrated at New York and Newport, while Washington's army of 11,000 men held the country north of New York and along the Hudson river. Occasionally the British, now commanded by Sir Henry Clinton, made some barbarous raids on the coasts of the New England States as well as of New Jersey, Virginia and the Carolinas. Washington was unable to repel these assaults, as any attempt to weaken his force, would have been the signal for Clinton to use his whole army to secure full control over the Hudson river. If such a coup de main would be successful, than all connection between the New England States and the South would be cut, and it would be easy for the British to subdue each part separately.

Well aware of such designs, the Americans had fortified several places on the river: West Point in the centre of the highlands, Stony Point on the west side, and Verplanck's with Fort Lafayette on the east bank. Between these two places ran King's Ferry, by which troops and provisions were taken across the river.

It was during the night of May 31, when the British sailed up the Hudson in an attempt to force the river. Clinton himself was to take Stony Point, while General Vaughan was to capture Verplanck's and Fort Lafayette. When the twenty men at Stony Point discovered Clinton's large force approaching, they fled, whereon Clinton took possession of the fort. Turning now its guns upon the Fort Lafayette, it was reduced in short time. Its garrison had to surrender, for General Vaughan had cut off their retreat.

To hold these important positions, Clinton set his soldiers at once to work to make Stony Point a formidable fortress, large enough to shelter a garrison of seven hundred men, well supplied with cannons, mounted to defend it on all sides.

Washington, greatly troubled by the enemy's success, decided to destroy the British fortifications at Stony Point at any cost. But as he had no troops to spare to make a regular attack, the fortress had to be taken by a surprise under cover of the night, as in day time the storming party would be exposed to the fire of the garrison as well as of the guns at Verplanck's across the river.

There was one general in the army who was well fitted for such a daring attempt: General Anthony Wayne, known to all soldiers by his nickname "Mad Anthony." When Washington did ask him if he would undertake such an enterprise, he answered, "I will storm hell, general, if you will only plan it."

After such plans had been made with the utmost care, Wayne was placed in command of twelve hundred selected men of light infantry. In the dark night of July 15, this force disembarked at some distance from Stony Point and divided into several storming parties, one of which began to assault the breastworks of the fort on its strongest side. While they drew the full attention of the British to this least vulnerable point, the main storming party, led by Wayne, suddenly hurled itself from the opposite direction up the steep sides of the hill with a dash which showed that the American soldiers, under Steuben's strict discipline, had now become seasoned fighters.

They had been forbidden to fire a single shot and were to rely upon their bayonets only. But their charge was so sudden and so fierce that to the completely surprised British nothing remained but to surrender. Here it was for the first time that the American troops met the disciplined British red-coats with the bayonet and brilliantly defeated them. 553 prisoners were taken. While the British had 63 killed, the loss of the Americans was 15 killed and 83 wounded. At two o'clock in the morning, Wayne wrote the following letter to General Washington:

"Stony Point, 16th July, 1779. 2 o'clock A. M.

Dear General! The fort and garrison, with Colonel Johnson, are ours. Our officers and men behaved like men who are determined to be free.

Yours most sincerely,

Anthony Wayne." ..

When on the next day Washington in company with Steuben inspected the place, they were not only greeted by their soldiers with enthusiasm, but assured, that from now on they would hold their bayonets in better regard than to roast beefsteaks with them, as they had done before.

After the fortifications at Stony Point had been destroyed, the Americans evacuated the place, whereon the British on July 22 again took possession of the rocky hill, but quitted it at the end of the year, without having made another effort to restore the fortress.

At this time Washington requested Steuben to give a written review of the whole military situation. Submitted on July 27, this review contains the following highly interesting remarks:

"Our present situation is about the same as it was at the commencement of the campaign. The enemy is still numerically superior. Their troops are better provided than ours. They are better able to carry out their

Uniforms of the American Army, 1779-1784
Light Infantry.

General	Privates
Colors: Blue faced with white and red.	Blue faced with white.

From plate VI of "Uniforms of the Army of the United States." Published by the Quartermaster General.

plans, and, on account of their ships, they are masters of the coast and of the mouth of the North or Hudson river.

"The taking of Stony Point was a great advantage for our side. It has not only encouraged the army but the people. It has shown the enemy that our generals know how to make a plan, and that our officers and soldiers know how to carry it out, with boldness and precision. It has delayed the field operations of the enemy but it has not altogether defeated their plans.

"Let us examine what those plans probably are. The great preparations which the enemy have made to protect themselves on both sides of the river at King's Ferry, the time, labor and expense they have employed in fortifying this point—can they have any other object than the burning and plundering the coasts of Connecticut? Would they have fortified Stony and Verplanck's Points to terminate their conquests there for this campaign? Neither supposition is at all probable. Their plans must be more comprehensive. Having fortified these two points, and leaving a sufficient garrison in them they are at liberty to take the rest of their forces wherever they think proper, and in a case of a reverse these two points are a support for their troops and a harbor for their vessels. They will then invade the country with a view to encouraging us to follow them by detachments, or with our full force, while they will be ready at any moment to make an attack on West Point with three or four thousand men and the vessels necessary for their transport. If, on the other hand, we do not allow ourselves to be drawn from our present position by their invasion, it is possible that they may send a corps of five or six thousand men, on either side of the river, to seem to threaten our flanks, and try to maneuver in our rear, so as to attack West Point. This, however, seems to me very difficult, particularly on the side of the fort.

"Whatever means they employ, I am positive that their operations are directed exclusively to getting possession of this fort, and of the river as far as Albany. If this is not their plan they have not got one worth the expense of a campaign. On their success depends the fate of America. The consequence is, therefore, that there is nothing of greater importance to us than to avert this flow. Let them burn what they have not burned already, and this campaign will add to their shame, but not to their success. Were West Point strongly fortified, supplied with sufficient artillery, ammunition and provision, and a garrison of two thousand men, we ought not to be induced to take our forces more than a day's march from it. To have the means of relieving it, I go further and say that our army should be destroyed or taken before we allow them to commence an attack on West Point. Were it possible to place a brigade or two somewhere between Sufferns and Fort Montgomery, the enemy would be compelled to keep more men and ships near Stony Point, and although I do not think it advisable to risk a second enterprise against the same point, I should wish the enemy to apprehend it . . .

"Let us defend North River and hold West Point, and the end of our campaign will be glorious. The above is my opinion on the present condition of affairs. The arrival of our ally's fleet on the coast would materially change our plan for operations."

As the British found the Americans always on the alert, they had in this part of the country no chance for a decisive operation, and so the summer passed away quietly. Meanwhile Steuben, to raise the army to still greater efficiency, kept up his drills. At the same time he enforced a rigid system of inspection by holding every man responsible for his arms, ammunition and outfit, and by insisting on strict accounting for everything ordered and delivered.

Let us hear, what Wm. North in his biographical sketch of Steuben said about these examinations:

"I have seen the Baron and his assistants seven long hours inspecting a brigade of three small regiments. Every man not present must be accounted for; if in camp, sick or well, they were produced or visited, every musket handled and searched, cartridge boxes opened, even the flints and cartridges counted; knapsacks unslung, and every article of clothing spread on the soldier's blanket, and tested by the little book, whether what he received from the United States within the year was there, if not, to be accounted for. Hospitals, stores, laboratories, every place and everything were opened to inspection, and inspected, and what officer's mind was at ease if losses or expenditures could not on the day of searching be fully and fairly accounted for? The inspections were every month, and wonderful was the effect, not only with regard to economy, but in creating a spirit of emulation between different corps?"

It was after the war, that Richard Peters, formerly chairman of the War Board, wrote the following letter to Alexander Garden: "Steuben's merits have never been duly appreciated. Our army was but a meritorious, irregular band before his creation of discipline. His department and personal conduct were particularly under my observation. One fact to prove his usefulness will go farther than a thousand words. In the estimate of the War Office we always allowed five thousand muskets beyond the actual numbers of our muster of the whole army. It was, in early times, never sufficient to guard against the waste and misapplication that occurred. In the last inspection returns of the main army, before I left the War Department, Baron Steuben being the inspector-general, only three muskets were deficient, and those accounted for."

While through such rigid inspection Steuben prevented waste and thus saved the government heavy expenses, his own financial situation grew worse from day to day. His compensation as Inspector-General was nominally $2,000 per year, but this was paid in Continental currency, or paper money, then almost worthless As he had to support out of this allowance not only himself, but his servants and horses, he suffered severely under those conditions. He even was compelled to take up loans, to meet the most pressing expenses. Several times Washington called the attention of Congress to this matter, asking that the Board of War might be authorized to grant to Steuben from time to time such amounts as were necessary.

"It is reasonable" so he wrote "that a man devoting his time and service to the public—and by general consent a very useful one—should at least have his expenses borne. His established pay is certainly altogether inadequate to this." . . .

But as usual, Congress delayed this matter for weeks and months. In the meantime Steuben's situation became so grave and perplexing that he considered asking for his discharge.

Hearing of his inclination Col. Benjamin Walker, greatly disturbed, wrote to Steuben the following letter:

"Your intention of quitting us cannot but give me much concern, both as an individual and as a member of the Commonwealth, convinced as I am of the necessity of your presence to the existence of order and discipline in the army. I cannot but dread the moment when such event shall take place, for much am I afraid we should again fall into the state of absolute negligence and disorder from which you have in some manner drawn us."

It was not before March 7, 1780 that Congress finally voted to give Steuben the sum of 250 Louisd'ors to reimburse him for the expenses of himself and his suite in coming to America, and to advance him the sum of 540 Louis d'ors.

That such fear, as expressed in North's letter, was not without foundation became evident only a few weeks later when a number of troops from Connecticut, encamped in Morristown, disclosed their contempt for Congress in open mutiny. They complained that they were "perpetually on the point of starving, were often entirely without food; were exposed without proper clothing to the rigors of the season, and now served almost twelve months without pay."

These complaints were only too well justified. While the State Legislatures never adjourned without paying themselves in full, and while those on the United States civil list received their salaries regularly, the army was always forgotten. The troops lived practically from hand to mouth, and food conditions were almost as bad as they had been at Valley Forge. In addition to these embarrassments came those caused by the worthlessness of the Continental paper money. Constantly it was going down. At the beginning of 1780 one paper dollar was equal to two cents in real money; before the end of 1780 it took ten paper dollars to make a cent. If paid in such paper money, butter cost twelve dollars a pound, a bushel of corn fifteen dollars, flour one thousand five hundred and seventyfive dollars a barrel. All other necessities of life were in proportion.

No wonder, that all other expressions of contempt, as for instance "not worth a farthing," or "not worth a tinker's dam," gave way to the new designation of worthlessness: "not worth a Continental!"

Continental Paper Money.

As the army was paid in such Continental paper money, if paid at all, the situation of the troops and officers was hard beyond description.

The first outbreak of mutiny was suppressed without great difficulty. But other acts followed soon. On the night of January 1, 1781 six regiments of Pennsylvania troops, numbering 1300 men, revolted and announced their intention to march to the seat of Congress to demand immediately their arrears of pay and clothing, that their pay should be "real pay", not worthless paper in the future, and that those troops who had served three years should receive their discharge.

General Wayne, the commander of these troops, during his efforts to hold these soldiers back was almost bayoneted. Congress, thoroughly frightened by the threatening situation, hurried a number of commissioners to the spot, who patched up a compromise, granting practically everything the mutineers demanded.

The natural consequence of this dangerous pact were other revolts. On January 20, 1781 the New Jersey troops attempted to follow the example of the Pennsylvanians. But now Washington ordered General Howe with a strong force to compel the mutineers to unconditional submission. This achieved, the most active and incendiary leaders were instantly executed.

In a general order, issued to the army Washington expressed his deep sympathy for the terrible hardships the troops were compelled to bear, but at the same time he exhorted them not to seek redress by flying in the face of law and government. "It is our duty to bear present evils with fortitude, looking forward to the period when our country will have it more in its power to reward our services."

But the spirit of revolt rose again in 1782, this time in the army of General Greene, after the troops of Pennsylvania had joined it. Again it was suppressed and the principal ringleaders tried, sentenced and shot.

Such revolts, however, were not the only demoralizing effects of these hard times. Again treason reared its head. We only need to mention the names of General Benedict Arnold and Major Andre, to recall in every American the story of that scoundrely act through which, if it had succeeded, West Point, the very citadel of the Revolution, would have been delivered into the hands of the enemy.

The Treason of Benedict Arnold.

West Point was to protect the ferrying of troops and supplies between New England and the other colonies. For this reason the place, made strong by nature, was fortified with walls of earth and logs, 14 feet high, and 21 feet wide at the base. It was 1800 feet around the main work. One hundred guns of various calibre were placed in the main fort and in the surrounding bastions and ditches. To prevent the passing of British vessels at night, a great iron chain, strengthened with a boom of pine logs, was stretched across the river. As the fort was so strong and conveniently situated, the army's main supplies of powder were stored here.

The possession of this stronghold would secure to the British full control of the Hudson river, facilitate intercourse between New York and Canada and would cut off the New England States from the rest of the country. For this reason the British were eager to get West Point at all means.

According to Channing the British headquarters had lists of such Americans, who were probably approachable. These lists contained also the degree of ease with which it was supposed these persons could be corrupted.

The person with whom Sir Henry Clinton, the British commander, made such a bargain, was General Benedict Arnold, a daring officer, but wanting in character. After the evacuation of Philadelphia by the British he had been entrusted with the office of a military commander of that city. While in this position he lived in great style and began to flirt with the remaining Tories of Philadelphia in a manner that gave occasion for much remark, especially when he became engaged to Margaret Shippen, the youngest daughter of Judge Shippen, a staunch Tory. At the same time a series of complaints were preferred against him, charging him with various transactions of a crooked nature.

But Arnold had among the members of Congress several influential friends, and so the court martial applied a thorough white-wash, acquitting him of all intentional wrong, reprimanding him for "imprudence" only.

In view of these occurrences it seems inconceivable that a man of such dubious character could be entrusted with the command of West Point, this all-important fortress, the loss of which would mean to the Americans death by decapitation.

It was through the influence of his friends, General Philip Schuyler and Robert R. Livingston, that Arnold sought and obtained the command of West Point. Arriving there on August 3, 1780, he established his headquarters not within the fort, but at the confiscated mansion of a Tory, Colonel Beverly Robinson, which was just below West Point, but on the opposite bank of the river.

From this secluded spot Arnold opened a secret correspondence with British headquarters at New York, signing his letters "Gustavus." These letters were answered by the adjutant of Sir Henry Clinton, Major John Andre, who used the pen-name "John Anderson."

While Arnold's treason and Andre's interception are mentioned more or less in all American histories, the real facts, however, are very little known. They are given here in full, as they illustrate by what heinous intrigues the success of the American War for independence was endangered.

To settle all details of the bargain, Arnold suggested a personal interview with Andre, naming September the 20th as the most convenient day, as then Washington would be on his way to meet the French general De Rochambeau at Hartford, Connecticut. Washington started on September 18th, accordingly Andre on September 20th went on board of the war sloop "Vulture", to proceed up the Hudson. He met Arnold at midnight of September 21, six miles below Stony Point. But as at dawn the negotiations between the conspirators had not been fully concluded, they went to the house of Joshua Hett Smith, a few miles further up the river. Hardly had they reached the house, when they heard the booming of cannons, and they saw, that the "Vulture" was fired upon by the Americans, who thought that the British vessel was too near their lines. Without delay the crew of the sloop hoisted anchor and sailed farther down the river.

Having taken breakfast together at Smith's house, the two conspirators completed the arrangements for the surrender of West Point. It was agreed upon that 30,000 guineas, about 150,000 dollars, and a major general's commission were to be the price for which West Point was to be turned over to the British. Furthermore, that at midnight of September 26, a strong British army would march to surprise the garrison of the fortress. Arnold would take care that in that night the American troops should be placed in squads in particular localities where they easily might be captured or slaughtered by the British. Furthermore Arnold would see that a link was taken out of the great chain across the river, so that, if a a British fleet were coming up, the sailors could quickly separate the boom, so that the two ends would swing round against the shores.

Arnold also furnished the British officer with exact plans of all the fortifications as well as with notes about their armament, the number of troops, etc. These papers, which were in Arnold's own handwriting, Andre concealed in his boots inside the stockings. Arnold then, in case Andre should not be able to reach the "Vulture" by water, gave him his own horse and the following pass:

"Headquarters Robinson House, Sept. 23, 1780.

Permit Mr. John Anderson to pass the guards to the White Plains, or below, if he chooses. He being on Public Business by my direction.

B. Arnold, M. General."

The interview ended, Arnold returned to his home, while Andre passed the day at Smith's house, expecting to go on board the "Vulture" at night. But as the owner of the house, fearing for his own safety, refused to put him on board, he decided to return to New York by land. Smith brought him to King's Ferry, where the ferry-man, well acquainted with Smith, took him across the river.

While on his solitary way, Andre encountered in the neighborhood of Tarrytown three men, the foremost of which wore a uniform like that of a German Yager in British service. Believing to be now within the British lines, Andre imprudently exclaimed:

"My lads, I hope you belong to our party!"

"What party?"

"The lower party!" said Andre.

"So do we," replied the leader of the three. Andre, thrown entirely off his guard, now declared himself to be a British officer, out of the country on particular business and eager to return to headquarters.

"You are our prisoner! shouted Paulding, the leader of the three, and refused to permit Andre to proceed, although he showed Arnold's pass and offered his gold watch, his horse, as well as a large amount of money, if they would release him. Instead the three men forced Andre to dismount. A thorough investigation of his clothes brought to light the papers, which stated the number of soldiers at West Point, as well as the number of guns and their position.

"By God, he is a spy!" exclaimed Paulding.

The men now conducted their prisoner to North Castle and surrendered him to Colonel Jameson. This simple-minded officer guilelessly ordered Lieutenant Allen with four men to escort the prisoner to the headquarters at West Point. A letter was to inform General Arnold that the documents, found on the prisoner, had been sent to Washington who was then on his way back from Connecticut. Lieutenant Allen had already started, when Major Tallmadge, a young cavalry officer, became aware of the grave blunder of his superior. Immediately the four soldiers with the prisoner were called back, while Lieutenant Allen proceeded to deliver the letter to Arnold.

The letter was delivered when Arnold with General Lafayette and some other officers sat at breakfast at his headquarters, the Robinson house.

"Excuse me, gentlemen!" he said, leaving the table, "some important business will require my attention for a few minutes. Please make yourselves at home meanwhile."

He then left the room, seized his holster with pistols and powder-flask, threw himself on the horse of one of his guests and dashed down the hill to the river. Here he jumped into a boat and commanded the oarsmen to take him as rapidly as possible to the "Vulture," the British man-of-war, riding at anchor eighteen miles down the river. So the traitor made his ignominous escape, without punishment.

Soon after Washington arrived from his journey. When he was informed of Arnold's conspiracy and flight, he was deeply shocked, as he had trusted Arnold for his bravery and military talents with great affection. Now he found, that this man, while in daily intercourse with his fellow soldiers, and while enjoying their friendship and sympathy, had been conspiring with the enemy, to betray the cause, for which they all had so often fought.

"Whom can we trust now?" the commander simply said, retiring to his room. But all the night through the guards could hear his steps, while he, lost in bitter thoughts, restlessly paced the floor.

Arnold arrived aboard the "Vulture" in New York on September 26. On October 7, he directed the following letter to Lord George Germain, the British Secretary of State for the Colonies:
                    "New York, 7th October, 1780.
My Lord:

"Conscious of the rectitude of my Intentions (whatever Constructions may have been put on my Conduct) and convinced of the benevolence and goodness of your

Lordship, I am emboldened to request Your Interest and Intercession, that I may be restored to the favor of my most gracious Sovereign; In the fullest Confidence of his Clemency, I most cheerfully cast myself at his feet, imploring his Royal Grace and Protection.

"I have that Confidence in the Goodness of Sir Henry Clinton, That His Majesty will not remain long uninformed that some considerable time has elapsed, since I resolved to devote my Life and Fortune to his Majesty's Service, and that I was intent to have Demonstrated my Zeal by an Act, which, had it succeeded as intended, must have immediately terminated the unnatural Convulsion that have so long distracted the Empire.

"Your Lordship will perceive by the enclosed address to the Public, by what principles I have been and am now actuated, to which I shall at present only add my most sacred Assurance that no endeavors of mine shall be wanting to confirm the Profession I make of an unalterable Attachment to the Person, Family and Interests of my Sovereign, and the Glory of his Reign. I enclose another Paper with some imperfect Notes, but will do myself the honor by the next Conveyance to transmit Your Lordship a more full and perfect State of Matters than in my present Confusion and Circumstance I am able to do.

"I shall endeavor to merit your Lordships Patronage by my Zeal and Assiduity in His Majesty's Service.

"I have the honor to be with the greatest Respect My Lord Your Lordships Most Obedient and most humble servant.

B. Arnold."

The originals of this document as well as of the paper mentioned in the letter, are in the English State Paper Office at London. As the paper describes the situation of the Americans at that time, as seen by an expert soldier, it is given here in full:

"THE PRESENT STATE OF THE AMERICAN REBEL ARMY, NAVY, AND FINANCES, WITH SOME REMARKS

"The present operating force under the immediate command of General Washington as stated by himself

to a Council of General Officers the 6th inst. amounts
to .... 10,400 men
One battalion of Continental troops at
Rhode Island 500
Two State Regiments of Continental militia
at North Castle 500

11,400 men

"About one-half of these troops are militia, whose time of service expires on the first day of January next, which will reduce the Army engaged for the war to less than six thousand men, exclusive of the troops in the Southern Department under General Gates, who may amount to eight hundred or a thousand regular troops besides militia; about 350 light horse are included in the above calculation. All these troops are illy clad, badly fed, and worse paid, having in general two or three years' pay due to them. Many of the best officers of the army have resigned, and others are daily following their example, through disgust, necessity, and a conviction that the Provinces will not be able to establish their independence.

"There has long subsisted a jealousy between Congress and the army. The former have been jealous of the power of the latter, and the latter have thought themselves neglected, and ill-treated by the former, who have excluded the Army from every appointment of honor, or profit in the civil line. The common soldier are exceedingly disgusted with the Service, and every effort to recruit the army (except by temporary draughts of militia), has hitherto proved ineffectual. Congress and General Washington last Spring made the most pressing demands on the Colonies to furnish a body of troops to complete the army to 35,000 men; every argument was urged to enforce the demand, among others that it would enable General Washington (in conjunction with the French troops) to oblige Sir Henry Clinton to evacuate New York—and thereby put a period to the war. The Colonies promised to comply with the requisition, every effort was used, but without success. The body of the people heartily tired of the war, refused to enlist voluntarily, and not more than one-third of the men ordered to be drafted, appeared in the field. The distress and discontents of the people are daily increasing, and the difficulty of recruiting the army another year will undoubtedly be greater than ever.

"The navy is reduced to three frigates, and a few small vessels, who are generally in port, for want of hands to man them.

"The treasury is entirely empty and the finances are at the lowest ebb. The public debt, inclusive of paper emitted by Congress, and the Colonies, Loan Office Certificates, and arrears due to the army, commissaries and quartermasters amounts to upwards of four hundred million paper dollars. Congress has lost all confidence and credit with the people, who have been too often deceived and duped by them to pay any regard to their promises in future; the different Provinces have very little more credit with the people than Congress. Their late emissions of paper, for the payment of which they have given every possible security, can hardly be said to have any currency, and is depreciating rapidly.

"As the result of their distress the eyes of the people are in general opened; they feel their error and look back with remorse to their once happy condition, and most ardently wish for a reconciliation on terms safe and honorable to both countries. Many would return to it with implicit confidence. Some doubt the sufficiency of the powers of the present commissioners to offer or accept terms for an established accommodation. It would serve very good uses if the commissioners have authority for it, to signify, that the Colonies upon returning to their obedience, shall be restored to their ancient condition with respect to their charter, rights, and privileges, civil and religious, free from British taxation, and to invite to negotiation for General Regulations. It will increase the number of advocates for the reunion.

"But the best step is to vest commissioners with decisive powers on such settlement as Great Britain may be willing to establish. There will always be jealousies seen while a power is reserved to Great Britain to approve or disapprove what her commissioners have done. With power in a set of commissioners to bind the nation as firmly as she would bind herself, by future acts of Parliament, I am of opinion that a pacification would immediately take place.

"But should the artful and designing who have assumed the reins of government, continue to have sufficient influence to mislead the minds of the people, and continue the opposition to government, I am clearly of opinion that an addition of ten thousand troops to the American Army (including those who may be on their way to America) will be a sufficient force under the direction of an officer of the experience and abilities of Sir Henry Clinton to put a period to the contest in the course of the next campaign.

"I have forgot to mention that the want of provision in the army is not owing to the scarcity of provision in the country, but to the weakness of the usurpation in every Colony, without money or credit supplies must be collected by force and terror, wherever the army are they take without opposition. But this force acts against itself by creating internal enemies, and by making friends to Great Britain. It is one of the principal saps hourly undermining the strength of the rebellion. N.B.—In the foregoing estimate the French troops at Rhode Island, who amount to about 5,000 effectives, are not included.

B. ARNOLD."

The "address to the public," mentioned in Arnold's letter to Lord Germain, is in fact an appeal to the American army to imitate his example. A copy of this proclamation, which was printed in New York, is in the Library of Congress, Division of Manuscripts. It is directed "To the officers and soldiers of the Continental army who have the real interest of their country at heart, and who are determined to be no longer the tools and dupes of Congress, or of France."

Then it says:

"His Excellency Sir Clinton has authorized me to

raise a corps of cavalry and infantry, who are to be clothed, subsisted, and paid as the other troops are in the British service, and those who bring in horses, arms, or accoutrements, are to be paid their value, or have liberty to sell them. To every non-commissioned officer and private a bounty of THREE GUINEAS will be given, and as the Commander-in-Chief is pleased to allow me to nominate the officers, I shall with infinite satisfaction embrace this opportunity of advancing men whose valor I have witnessed, and whose principles are favorable to a union with Britain, and TRUE AMERICAN LIBERTY.

"The rank they obtain in the King's service will bear a proportion to their former rank, and the number of men they bring with them. It is expected that a Lieutenant Colonel of cavalry will bring with them 75 men, major of horse 50 men, captain 30, lieutenant 15, cornet 12, sergeant 6, a lieutenant colonel of infantry 75 men, major 50, etc. Each field officer will have a company."

In the second part of this document Arnold seeks to vindicate his own conduct and to impress his former comrades with the advantages they will gain by following his example. While this part is very ably composed, it failed, however, to produce the slightest effect.

There is little more to tell. Every effort was made by Sir Henry Clinton to save Andre's life. But Washington appointed a court-martial of fourteen of the highest officers, among them Steuben, to examine into the case of Andre. The sentence was given unanimously on September 29, according to which Andre on October 2 had to undergo a felon's death. In regard to Andre's fate Steuben said afterwards: "It was not possible to save him. He put us to no proof, but in an open, manly manner confessed everything but a premeditated design to deceive. Would to God the wretch who drew him to death could have suffered in his place."

Steuben's abhorrence of Arnold's treason becomes evident by an incident preserved by Pomeroy Jones in his "History of Oneida County, N. Y."

"On one occasion after the treason the Baron was on parade at roll call when the detested name Arnold was heard in one of the infantry companies of the Connecticut line. The Baron immediately called the unfortunate possessor to the front of the company. He was a perfect model for his profession: clothes, arms and equipments in the most perfect order. The practiced eye of the Baron soon scanned the soldier, and "call at my marquee, after you are dismissed, brother soldier," was his only remark. After Arnold was dismissed from parade, he called at the Baron's quarters as directed. The Baron said to him "you are too fine a soldier to bear the name of a traitor, change it at once, change it at once!" "But what name shall I take " replied Arnold. "Any that you please. Take mine, if you cannot suit yourself better, mine is at your service!" Arnold at once agreed to the proposition, and immediately repaired to his orderly, and Jonathan Steuben forthwith graced the company roll, in lieu of the disgraced name of him who had plotted treason to his country.

"After the war, Jonathan Steuben returned to his native state Connecticut, where he married. His first son he named Frederick William, who fought in the war of 1812. He was orderly sergeant of his company, and with the name of the Baron he seems to have inherited at least a portion of his distinguished qualifications, for he was considered one of the best disciplinarians in his regiment."

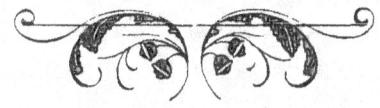

Steuben's Eventful Campaign in Virginia.

As if all the embarrassments related in the former chapter were not enough there came from the South most alarming tidings. The British had succeeded in taking two important cities of South Carolina, Charleston and Camden. The 3,000 Continental troops, stationed at Charleston, had surrendered at Camden. The army of General Gates' was captured, sloughtered or scattered. The gallant General De Kalb was killed, while Gates had saved himself by a flight so hasty, that he arrived at night in Charlotte, 80 miles from the battlefield. What to do now in face of this grave situation, was a serious question.

In Washington's Council of War Steuben was probably the most competent person. Before preparing for a new campaign the commander-in-chief requested Steuben frequently not only to draw up a general review of the situation, but also to suggest plans for the kind of actions that should be taken.

Such was now the case. In response to Washington's request Steuben on September 10, 1780, submitted the following memorial:

"Upon a general view of the situation, and especially after the unhappy affair to the southward, I think that our only object should be to stop the progress of the enemy till some more fortunate events permit us to act on our part. To do this I would not only wish the army to be kept together, but I should wish for as speedy as possible a junction with the French troops. What appears to me most likely is, that the enemy, after the defeat of General Gates, will endeavor to push their conquest to the southwest, and being sure that we are not able to undertake anything against New York, they will embark what troops can be spared, and make a descent on Virginia, where there is nothing but militia to oppose their progress. How to stop them in that quarter is the most difficult to answer. The successive detachments we have already sent has lost us the troops of six states. Always inferior to the enemy, and not supported by the provincials or militia, they have been sacrificed as fast as they have been sent. Can we risk now to expose the Pennsylvania line to the same fate? At any rate we can not before the junction of the French troops with our army.

"To attempt to retake by detachments of our army what we have lost in that quarter, we shall in the end be defeated by detail. I could cite many examples where whole armies have been defeated by detachment. Prince Eugene, against the French, risked his reputation and the loss of the house of Austria for having weakened his army by detachment—he was totally defeated by detail. But our own experience will suffice. The troops of six states have already been lost, and if these states cannot or will not replace their troops the State of New Hampshire would at least be left to defend the whole thirteen states. To detach any part of the army at present seems to me of more dangerous consequences than any progress the enemy can make to the southward. In fact they can only ravage the country, and this we cannot hinder even with a superior force; and should they take possession of any places on the coast, so soon as the maritime forces of our allies become superior to theirs on the coast they must abandon them.

"The greatest danger, in my opinion, that can threaten the country is a defeat of our army. The disaffected would become discouraged and all our resources become more difficult. We should even in that case lose every advantage that we might reap from the arrival of a fleet of our allies to our assistance. My opinion then is absolutely this, to play a sure game, and rather suffer some little insult than risk the whole; to keep our army together as much as possible, and prepare ourselves to act with vigor when our allies come to our assistance."

In concluding this memorial, the correctness of which was manifested in the future, Steuben asserted that the only assistance that could possibly be given to the Southern States, was to delegate two able officers to take charge of the situation. Now, when Washington appointed his most reliable officer Major-General Nathaniel Greene for this difficult job, what wiser plan could he have followed than to send Steuben with him? Steuben had served before as confidential adviser to General Robert Howe, while he was in command at West Point and when it was seriously treated by the British. With Greene Steuben was on the most friendly terms; both were above petty jealousies, and both were inspired with enthusiasm for the great cause they had sworn to.

While on their journey, the two generals had ample time to consider the plans to be pursued. They came to the conclusion that, to save Virginia it was necessary to break the British forces in the Carolinas. But as the number of reliable troops in the Carolinas was much too small, it was decided that Steuben should remain in Virginia to collect whatever men and means might be gathered and to send them to Greene, who was to take charge of the campaign in the Carolinas.

The work, Steuben had to perform, was embarrassing to the extreme as the general conditions in Virginia were almost as bad as those he had faced in the North in 1778.

Fragments of a former army still existed, but they were scattered over the whole state, and none of these detachments was in possession of arms, ammunition, food or clothing. In addition, the National idea was as yet imperfectly realized. It was here as elsewhere that, when the British invaded a section of the country, the yeomanry troops of that section would flock to repel the enemy, but go home again, as soon as the danger had passed. That decisive results and final victory could be achieved only if all the inhabitants of the States would pull together to the one end was a lesson to be learned yet.

Consequently Steuben experienced great difficulty in overcoming the indifference of the people as well as the reluctance of the Assembly of Virginia, when he asked not only for the State's quota of 3,000 troops, thoroughly equipped, but also for the establishment of a magazine of 10,000 barrels of flour, 5,000 barrels of pork and beef, 3,000 head of cattle, 200 hogshead of rum, and many other things; not forgetting a military chest with 5,000 pounds of real cash ($25,000) to meet current expenses. Such a demand had never been made before, and as the greater part of the men as well as of the provisions were to be sent out of the State, to the Carolinas, there arose everywhere hot discussion and clamor of dissatisfaction.

To re-inforce the small army of General Greene with as many troops as possible was a job difficult beyond belief. In the first place the fragments of the former army that were roaming over all sections of Virginia had to be collected. But when the first detachment, summoned to Richmond appeared in that city, it became evident, that these so-called troops had utterly lost all sense of discipline and duty; besides, they were so deficient in clothing, and so dirty, that they could not be accepted in such condition. They arrived 378 strong, but when Steuben gave orders to march to North Carolina, 41 of these men disappeared during the night. And on the next morning their commander, General Lawson, produced an order of the Legislature, to discharge all these men. As this order was verified the next day by Governor Thomas Jefferson, nothing remained but to comply.

More fortunate was Steuben with a detachment under the command of General Peter Muehlenberg, formerly pastor at Woodstock. Va. His corps had 900 men, of whom Steuben selected 400 to be sent at once to Greene. On December 3rd however, a delegation of the officers informed Steuben of their unability to march until certain complaints against the State for ill usage had been righted and the equipment of the men brought in good order. As Steuben promised to attend to their complaints, and as he succeeded in providing proper equipments, he was able to send Greene a detachment of 456 men. While the task of bringing such former soldiers into the ranks again was a permanent struggle with difficulties, it was still harder to collect sufficient numbers of recruits and make them real soldiers. In addition Steuben was constantly compelled to impress the Assembly of Virginia with the necessity of clothing their troops, as otherwise these men would fall victims to disease and death.

Headley, the well known historian, says that Greene during his campaign in the Carolinas relied entirely on regulars, such as Steuben sent him. "At Guiford a single regiment of such regulars broke two British regiments, each larger than itself, to pieces, without stopping to breathe. And at Eutaw Springs, although the militia fought nobly, the finishing blow was given by the Continentals, who swept the field with the bayonets, and to the utter amazement of the English troops, beat them with their favorite weapon."

While engaged in such tedious and worrying work, Steuben suddenly was startled by the information that on December 31, a British fleet of 19 ships, 2 brigs and 10 schooners had entered the mouth of the James river, the principal water course of Virginia. These vessels carried 1600 troops under command of Benedict Arnold, the traitor, who longed to demonstrate his abilities to Clinton, his new commander-in-chief, as well as to take revenge on his former associates.

As this meant another invasion of Virginia by a ruthless, brutal enemy, and as all available troops and recruits had been sent to North Carolina to re-enforce Greene, the whole population of Virginia became panic-stricken.

Steuben hurried to face the desperate situation as well as circumstances would permit. First, he took proper measures for the quick removal of all stores of provisions and ammunition, that had been established along the river. At the same time he increased, by herculean efforts his forces of militia men to such an extent, that he was able to harass the enemy during his raiding expedition up the river. While he was unable to prevent the devastation of a number of settlements and of Richmond, the capital, he succeeded in confining such ravages to a limited territory, and when Arnold retreated, Steuben immediately followed after—making a demonstration wherever there was the slightest chance of even partial success.

After the enemy's return to the ships Steuben established his headquarters at Smithfield, northwest of Plymouth. Other detachments under General Muehlenberg and General Lawson occupied the north bank of the James River. By these movements Steuben successfully prevented Arnold from making another incursion up the river. And as the arrival of a strong French fleet was expected at any moment, he entertained strong hope, that Benedict Arnold be bottled up in the mouth of the river, and made prisoner. Such an eventuality was not beyond possibility, as Washington had hurried a strong army of regular troops, commanded by Lafayette to Virginia, to come to the rescue. This army, was expected to arrive soon. And when, on March the 20th, a large fleet was seen entering Chesapeake Bay the success of the jubilant Americans seemed complete.

But alas! When these vessels showed their colors, they were not French but British. The flotilla, commanded by Admiral Arbuthnot, had defeated the French squadron sixty miles off the entrance of the bay.

By the arrival of this fleet the British troops were increased to 3,500 men, far too strong a force to be prevented from other marauding raids.

Again Steuben was compelled to confine his efforts to the saving of the stores of provision and arms, and again he had to retreat inch by inch into the interior of the State, unable to risk with his poorly equipped militia men a battle against such overwhelming odds. In a report sent on April the 15th to Washington, Steuben gave the following description of his status:

"My situation is not the most agreeable, as I am obliged to undertake the defence against more than three thousand regular troops with nothing to oppose them but militia, whose numbers decrease every day. Those who have served since the beginning of the invasion have discharged themselves and are not replaced by others, in consequenc of which General Muehlenberg is left on the south side of the James river with only seven

American Settlers Defending Their Homes.

hundred men, and General Weedon on the northside with about six hundred men. If the enemy have any intention to penetrate the country, the opposition we can make will avail little.

"A very great evil resulting from the invasion is, that it stops recruiting for the army. So long as a county has any militia in the field, so long that county is prevented from drafting, and as most of the counties have had part of their militia either here or with General Greene, little or nothing has been done in the business. Only fifty-two have yet come in, and of these some have already deserted."

A large division of the enemy, commanded by Lord Cornwallis, started on April the 16th, for another raid. There were twenty-five flat boats, each carrying one hundred men. Slowly ascending the James river the incendiaries destroyed all tobacco warehouses, vessels, and settlements on both banks of the river. Then entering the Appomatox, they continued in their work of devastation, setting everything in flames, and carrying off all objects of value.

Steuben could not risk a stand, as a defeat would have had fatal consequences for the whole state. Therefore he repeated his former tactics, evading open skirmishes, but annoying the enemy as much as possible.

To defend their homes against the brutal enemy, many settlers took part in such hot skirmishes, quite often assisted by their women and children.

These maneuvers were kept up during May and the first half of June, until Steuben was able on June the 19th to join Lafayette's army. As by this junction the American force was increased to five thousand men, the British were compelled to retreat, as otherwise they would risk being cut off from their ships.

It was now, that Cornwallis made that grave blunder which in the course of events delivered him into the hands of the Americans. Realizing, that the mouth of the James river was not a safe place for the British vessels, as they might easily be bottled up by a superior French fleet, he transfered his headquarters to Yorktown and Gloucester Point, two villages at the mouth of the York river. Here the broad sheet of the Chesapeake Bay promised greater security against a surprise by a hostile squadron.

But Cornwallis had hardly settled down in these quarters, when on September 5th the French Admiral De Grasse, coming from the West Indies, appeared with twenty-four vessels in Chesapeake Bay to give battle to the British fleet. The engagement, beginning on September 7, lasted for several days, ending with the total defeat of the British ships, of which only few succeeded in escaping to New York.

While now the French fleet held full control over the whole bay, the American troops under Steuben, Lafayette and Muehlenberg began to blockade the British army from the land side. Too late Cornwallis perceived that he was in a trap, with no hope for escape. And when on September 14th Washington and the French General Rochambeau appeared with several thousand men in the American camp at Williamsburg, everybody was convinced that a most decisive event in the war was near.

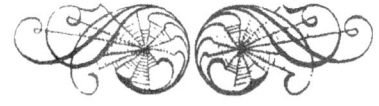

Steuben's Part in the Siege of Yorktown.

In these eventful days Yorktown was a village of about 60 houses with 400 inhabitants. Situated on a high bluff on the south bank of York river, about 12 miles from its mouth, it was a point of strategic value, as the bluff toward the interior formed a level plateau, embraced by deep ravines on either side.

Cornwallis after his arrival immediately had entered upon the work of fortification. His line of works completely surrounded the village and were well calculated to impede the approach of the enemy.

As Steuben was the only American general who ever had participated in the siege of a fortress—Schweidnitz—during the Seven Years' War, his experience was of special value.

It has even been said that the plans for the siege of Yorktown were prepared by him, a statement that unfortunately cannot be verified at the present time, as all official documents, relating to the siege of Yorktown were lost in a fire that in 1800 destroyed the office of the War Department.

Complying with Steuben's request for a regular command, Washington gave him the first division, composed of the Pennsylvania regiments, two regiments of Maryland and a regiment of Virginia. In all this force numbered 2,309 men. Its position was in the right center.

The first week in October was devoted by the allies to a thorough reconnoissance of grounds, the making of fascines, gabions and stakes, the bringing up of heavy guns, and other necessary preparations for a siege.

There was really but little fighting. The first trenches were begun during the night of October the 5th. The work made such progress, that in the morning of October 8th the bombarding of Yorktown could be opened. It resulted in the destruction of many buildings and several ships, which caught fire. In the evening of October 11th Steuben's division commenced the second parallel only three hundred and sixty yards distant from the British lines, under a very heavy fire of the enemy's batteries. Nevertheless the work was carried on with such amazing rapidity and dexterity, that in the morning the besiegers were able to open fire from their new positions. All efforts to dislodge the Americans failed.

There happened during this siege an incident well worth mentioning. One day Steuben and General Wayne, while observing the enemy, were standing in one of the trenches, when suddenly a shell crashed down within immediate neighborhood. To escape the effect of its explosion, Steuben threw himself on the ground of the trench. Wayne, following his example, fell on top of him. "Well," remarked Steuben laughing, "I always was aware of your fidelity as a soldier, but did not know that you would cover my retreat in such a perfect manner!"

When on October the 17th, Cornwallis raised the white flag of surrender, Steuben's regiments held the most advanced trenches in the center. The letter, proposing a suspension of hostilities for twenty-four hours to arrange the terms of surrender, was received by Steuben and by him forwarded to Washington.

Col. William North relates in his biographical sketch of Steuben (printed in the Magazine of American History) a peculiar incident that followed now:

"At the relieving hour next morning the Marquis de Lafayette approached with his division, but the Baron refused to be relieved, assigning as a reason the etiquette in Europe, that the offer to capitulate had been made during his guard, and that it was a point of honor of which he would not deprive his troops, to remain in the trenches till the capitulation was signed, or hostilities recommenced. The dispute was referred by Lafayette to the commander-in-chief; but Steuben remained until the British flag was struck."

Steuben's troops were the first who on October the 19th, entered Yorktown. Theirs was the honor of unfurling the beautiful flag of the victorious United States of America. Steuben was also specially mentioned along with generals Lincoln, Knox, Lafayette and others in the order issued by the commander-in-chief the day after the capitulation.

According to a diary, kept by one of the Hessian soldiers in the army of Cornwallis, "it was on the afternoon of the 19th of October, between the hours of 4 and 5 o'clock, that all the captured troops, with arms and baggage, standards covered but drums beating, marched out of their camps.

"The French who formed the right wing, had some richly dressed "heiducks" (fancy servants) in their suite, who being very tall and handsome men presented quite a dazzling appearance in their gold and silver laced liveries. All the French generals wore glittering stars and badges of military orders.

"On the right wing of each French regiment was gorgeously paraded a rich standard of white silk with three golden fleur de lis embroidered upon it. Beyónd these standards stood the drummers and fifers, and in front of them the band which played delightfully. It must be confessed that the French troops, altogether, looked very well; they were all tall, handsome men. They all wore gaiters; a part of them were clad in red, some also in green, most of them, however, were in white regimentals. The German, or Alsatian regiments had blue regimentals.

"The left wing of the line through which we had to march was formed of the Americans; in front of them their generals, Washington, Steuben, Gates and Wayne. They were paraded in three lines, the first composed of the regulars, who had also a band, playing moderately well. They looked passable; but the militia from Virginia and Maryland, forming the second and third lines, were both a ragged set of fellows and very ill looking."

The British army that surrendered here, consisted of 7247 troops and 840 sailors, 552 men were killed and wounded during the siege. The American and French forces consisted of 5000 Continental troops, 3500 militia men and 7,000 French soldiers or about 16,000 in all.

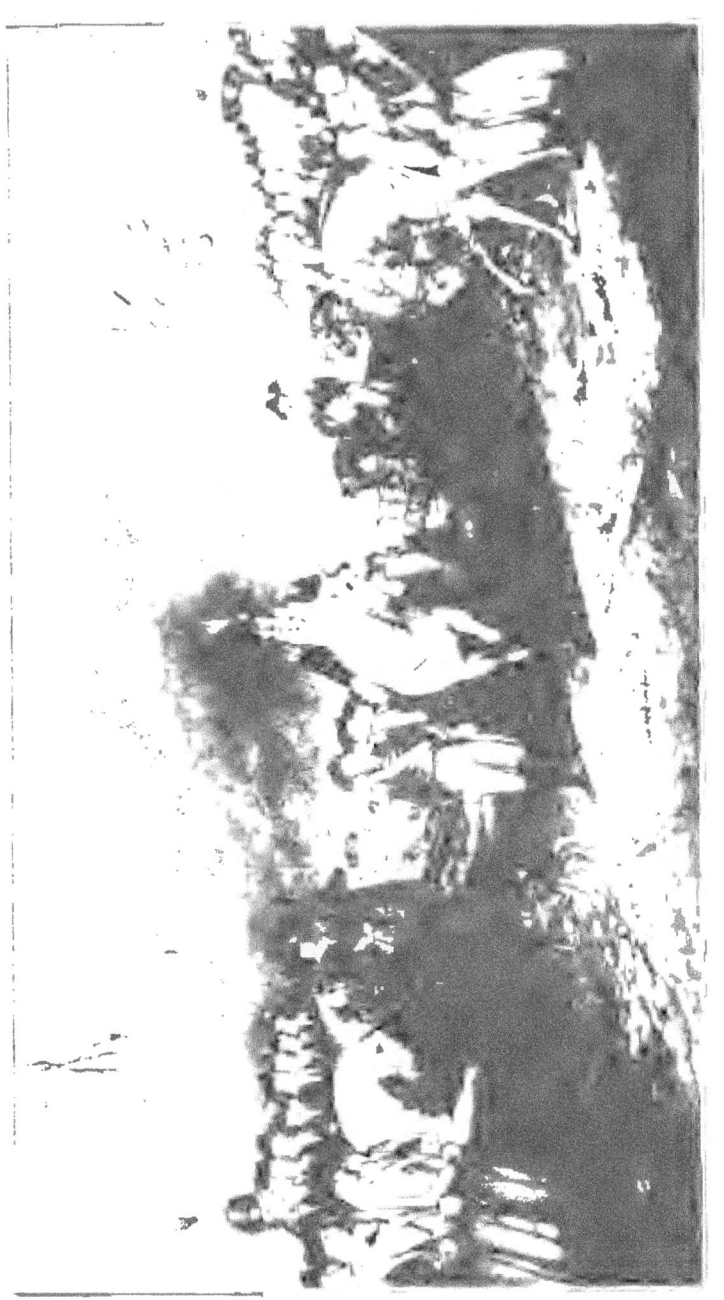

The Surrender of Cornwallis at Yorktown.

From the original painting by John Trumbull in the Capitol at Washington.

The loss was about 300 men killed and wounded. While these figures are very insignificant in comparison to those of the great battles of the 19th and 20th century, the siege of Yorktown nevertheless stands among the most decisive events in history.

The Most Critical Period in American History.

After the eventful days at Yorktown Steuben remained for some time in Virginia, to straighten out matters there. In the beginning of the year 1782 he joined again Washington's army at Newburgh, New York, to resume his manyfold duties as inspector-general. While the commander-in-chief had taken headquarters at a house on the west side of the Hudson river, where he was in a position to overlook the river for eight miles to West Point, Steuben's headquarters were on the east side of the river. From here he frequently crossed over to drill the various contingents of the troops as well as Washington's bodyguard. The members of the latter received instructions in all military tactics, with a view to making officers of them, in case the war should continue.

General Otho Williams, when visiting West Point in 1782 was deeply impressed with the change in the condition of the troops, and wrote to Steuben the following lines: "How much our troops are indebted to you, Sir, for that military ability and appearance in which they now both so advantageously compare with the best disciplined troops in Europe, Congress, his Excellency General Washington and other eminent characters, bear honorable testimony. The personal knowledge I have, as an officer of the American army, acquired from your general instructions, influences my gratitude to add my private thanks to the more important acknowledgments you have already and repeatedly received."

Wm. North, Steuben's aide-de-camp, relates in his notes (American Magazine of History 1882) that also the French officers, who frequently visited Steuben, were surprised at the perfection of discipline he had secured. "The Marquis Montmorency was especially struck at the silence with which these troops performed all their evolutions, and remarked upon it, saying he was surprised to hear so little noise. "Noise!" exclaimed Steuben, "I do not know where the noise should come from, when even my brigadiers dare not open their mouths, but to repeat my orders!" "Ah! hah! Monsieur le Baron" vociferated the Marquis, "je vous comprend! je vous comprend!" The French troops were exceedingly noisy in their evolutions and marches, and the Marquis was heard louder than the rest."

While Colonel North never tires of praising Steuben's uncomparable efficiency as drillmaster, John James Thacher in his "Military Journal of the American Revolutionary War" (Boston, 1823) has handed down to posterity the following example of Steuben's high sense of justice.

"At a review a lieutenant Gibbons was arrested and ordered to the rear for a fault which, it afterward appeared, another had committed. At a proper moment the commander of the regiment came forward and informed the Baron of Mr. Gibbon's innocence and of his acute feelings under his unmerited disgrace. "Desire Lieutenant Gibbons to come to the front, colonel." "Sir" said the Baron, addressing the young gentleman, "the fault which was committed by throwing the line into confusion might in the presence of an enemy have been fatal; I arrested you as its supposed author, but I have reason to believe that I was mistaken, and that in this instance you were blameless. I ask your pardon; return to your command, I would not deal injustly toward any one, much less toward one whose character as an officer is so respectable." All this passed with the baron's hat off, the rain pouring on his venerable head! Do you think there was an officer or soldier who saw it, unmoved by affection and respect? Not one."

At this time Steuben's "Regulations," the famous "Blue Book," had been printed and distributed among the officers of the army. To make sure, that its instructions would be properly carried out, Steuben suggested that in the future his department should have one inspector general, assisted by two inspectors, one for the army of the North and one for the army of the South. This proposition received the full approval of the commander-in-chief, and on January the 10th, the sanction of Congress. As by this act Steuben was vested with full power to appoint such officers as were necessary to carry his plans into execution, he made Colonel Stewart inspector for the northern army, and Lieutenant Colonel Jean Baptiste Ternant for the southern army. The latter had accompanied Steuben from France to America, and had done good service in Georgia and South Carolina.

While the surrender of Cornwallis at Yorktown had greatly relieved the Americans, the war was not yet ended. The city of New York was still in the hands of the enemy. And the British fleet, strongly reinforced recently, had beaten the French squadron in the West Indies and was again in full control of the Ocean. So the situation remained grave.

Eager to bring the war to a favorable end as soon as possible, Washington requested Steuben again to review the situation. Especially was he anxious to hear his opinion as to whether an attack on New York might promise success or would be too risky.

Accordingly Steuben prepared a resume of the state of affairs. Comparing the British forces with those of the Americans, he found that the enemy had 15,700 troops at his disposal, while the Northern Continental army numbered only 10,000 and the Southern army only 2,000. To these forces about 4,000 French troops might be added. With these figures at hand, Steuben explained the situation as follows:

"The position of the enemy in New York is on three islands. Whenever we attack one of these islands the other two must be kept in check. If then, the besieged should consist of 12,000 men, and the besiegers of 24,000, the latter must be divided into three parts, each consisting of 8,000 men. The points of attack are the passage of Kingsbridge, the Heights of Brooklyn and the works on Staten Island. The shortest line of communication between them is from 20 to 24 miles, with a river between each. How, then, is the one to support the other in case of a superior attack, which the enemy may easily make, as they possess every possible advantage by water? And even supposing we should obtain possession of either island, what position should we take to cover our flanks from the enemy's force by water? But if we should be unfortunate enough to have any one division defeated, what retreat is left while the enemy keep possession of the water?

"These reasons alone prove to me sufficiently the impropriety of such an undertaking as long as the enemy keep possession of the port and the river by which the islands are surrounded.

"As soon as a superior fleet shall have blocked up the harbor without, our principal object, I conceive will be Long Island, in which case the greater part of our strength will be necessarily employed in carrying the works at Brooklyn, either by storm or regular approaches, and to erect batteries to bombard the city and the fleet in the bay. But even then it will be necessary that our frigates should be in possession of the Sound, and the batteries should be erected on our flanks commanding the river.

"The last proposition supposes that we were in possession of the harbor and had the superiority at sea. In this case we should be highly reprehensible if we did not make the attempt; yet even then I would propose that we should have the most pointed assurances that the fleet destined for this service should remain long enough to effect a co-operation on the occasion. It would also be necessary to make an exact estimate of the number of troops and the means which we possess to make the attempt. If the enemy should abandon the southern States and collect their whole force at New York, it would amount to 16,000 men, and by recalling our troops thence we should amount to the same number. If they retain possession of Charlestown and Savannah, General Greene must also remain there, and then we shall be in the same proportion of 14,000 to 14,000.

"It would be no less difficult than hazardous to attack the enemy in their present position with less than double this number, or 28,000 men. If the States of Hampshire, Rhode Island, Connecticut, New York and

Jersey could send 4,000 men as rank and file into the regular army, it would amount to 14,000 men (Continental troops); 4,000 French and 10,000 militia; with this and no less than this, I conceive we might attempt the enterprise."

Concluding, Steuben showed conclusively that the hope of attacking New York successfully was chimerical, as it was improbable to collect and sustain a force sufficient to carry on a siege, all the more as the French fleet, lately defeated, would be unable to give assistance.

That Steuben's views were correct became evident soon enough. After the fall of Yorktown everybody was convinced that peace was near, and that no further exertions were necessary to secure this end. Consequently, there was a general relaxation of effort to maintain the army numerically at its height. And to support this army properly was always the very last consideration Congress had at heart.

The latter fact became evident during the winter of 1781 to 1782, when the conditions of the army assumed such a serious aspect that the officers as well as the soldiers grew extremely indignant at the neglect of Congress to pay them their dues and provide for their wants. It was during this period that Washington was approached by a group of officers, headed by Colonel Lewis Nicola, demanding that he send Congress home and institute another form of government, with himself as dictator or king.

The following sharp letter to the Secretary of War shows Washington's feelings during these times:

"Under present circumstances, when I see such a number of men goaded by a thousand stings of reflections on the past and anticipations of the future about to be turned into the world, soured by penury and by what they call the ingratitude of the public, involved in debts, without one farthing of money to carry them home after having spent the flower of their days, and many of them their patrimonies, in establishing the freedom and independence of their country, and suffering everything that human nature is capable of enduring on this side of death—I repeat it—when I consider these irritating circumstances, without one thing to soothe their feelings or dispel their prospects, I can not avoid apprehending that a train of evils will follow of a very serious and distressing nature. You may rely upon it, the patriotism and long-suffering of this army are well-nigh exhausted, and there never was so great a spirit of discontent as at this instant. While on the field I think it may be kept from breaking into acts of outrage; but when we retire into winter-quarters, unless the storm is previously dissipated, I cannot be at ease respecting the consequences. It is high time for peace."

That this dark picture was not exaggerated is proven by the fact that at the end of the year 1782 there was owing to the army $5,625,618. Another amount of $5,000,000 was due as commutation of the half-pay for life that had been granted by Congress to the officers at a time when there were no other means to keep these men in the service of the country.

Among all the poor sufferers encamped at Newburgh and its surroundings, Steuben without question was in the worst plight. While Washington and a number of the officers enjoyed independent resources, he had nothing to depend on. And so his financial conditions caused him always endless embarrassments. When during the siege of Yorktown the French officers vied with each other in acts of civility and attention to the American officers, giving in succession entertainments to them, Steuben was compelled to sell his favorite charger to obtain funds that he might return these acts of hospitality. "We are, God knows, miserably poor!" so he complained, "We are constantly feasted by the French without giving them even a bit of bratwurst. I can stand it no longer. Take my silver spoons and forks and sell them; I will give on grand dinner to our allies, should I eat my soup with a wooden spoon forever after!" At the same time, when Wm. North, his aide-de-camp, fell sick, he sold his watch to pay the doctor and for the medicine.

At the beginning of March (1782) Congress owed Steuben 6850 dollars in specie. Being unable to borrow any money he was again compelled to ask Washington for his mediation. His letter speaks for itself:

"Without troubling your Excellency with a tedious detail of the hardships attending my situation, I pray you to consider the peculiarity of my employment compared with that of other officers. The arrangements which are going to take place for furnishing the army with provisions, forage, etc., will not be of advantage to me, as I am bound to travel from one part of the country to the other, to live at double expenses in taverns, in which I have to pay ready money not only for my personal expenses, but also for the entertainment of my aides-de-camp and horses necessary to perform our journeys. I would be happy if the pay allowed by Congress were equal to such expenses. I do not want to lay up any part of my pay; I ask no addition to it. but I declare it to be totally out of my power if my appointments, as well those of January and February, as those occurring in the future, are not regularly paid me. With regard to the arrearages, I shall be satisfied to leave in the public funds $6,000, provided I am paid the remaining $850, which are indispensably necessary to enable me to discharge my expenses here and provide myself with the necessary equipage for the ensuing campaign."

Washington took the matter up at once with the effect that Steuben obtained the $850 he had asked for. Also $500 due for January and February. For the remaining $6,000 he accepted a certificate acknowledging that the United States owed to him that amount for arrears. As many debts as well as running expenses had to be paid the above pittance, received from Congress, melted away more quickly than snow exposed to hot sunshine. And so the old trouble soon began again. Despairing of his fate, Steuben one day wrote:

"If my life depended on it I would not be able to raise ten dollars on credit. The certificate for $6,000 which I hold from the United States I offered in vain for one-tenth of its nominal value. There is no resource whatever left in me. I have already lost six horses since I am in the service chiefly for want of forage. The two best were stolen, as, while in West Point, I had to send them twenty miles from that place to find pasturage for them. Besides that, for want of bolts and bars for my house, my silver and linen were stolen, so that I am reduced in everything."

It was in June, 1782, when Steuben by bitter want was compelled to direct to the Secretaries of War and Finance the following letter:

"While other officers were stationed within their respective divisions, brigades and corps, and could avail themselves of their ordinary supplies, the nature of my duty kept me in constant motion from one division of the army, and even from one army to another, necessarily subjecting me to all the expenses incident to traveling. I ever have been, and ever will be disposed to draw an equal lot with those truly brave men whose sufferings have long since called aloud for speedy redress; with them I have frequently wanted not only the conveniences but even the necessaries of life, and if my duty confined me to my camp and quarters, I would not conceive myself entitled to any extraordinary privilege. Hitherto I have never made a requisition of any kind to Congress, and entreat your Excellency to be persuaded that it is with singular pain I am compelled to make one at this time; but the duty I owe to my own feelings, as well as the respect I entertain to that august body, required that I should thus be explicit with them."

The Proceedings in Congress, relating to Steuben, show that on a motion made on July 26th, it was agreed that Steuben should receive in addition to his pay as major-general, 80 dollars per month for his traveling expenses in the execution of his office as inspector-general. But it does not appear that this money was ever paid. So Steuben resolved to go to Philadelphia to present his claims personally.

Inspecting the various divisions of troops, stationed along the line of his journey, he arrived in Philadelphia during the month of August. But here he had to bear all the depressing mortifications, such unfortuate persons had to suffer, who hoped for a quick consideration of their affairs by Congress. Week after week, month after month passed without his claims being taken up. Hearing of this unworthy treatment, Wm. North, deeply disgusted, wrote on October 29th the following letter to Steuben:

"Your services to my ungrateful country have been treated with a neglect shocking to every man of sensibility. The army of the United States knows what you have done; your intimate friends only know what you have suffered since you took the Herculean task of forming the American armies. It is now five years since you undertook this last work. How well you have succeeded the present state of the army will declare; but unfortunately for our honor your reward only consists in the consciousness of having acted a great and good part. The war, my dear general, is perhaps drawing towards a close. It has happily been successful, and you doubtless have acquired a lasting honor by the part you had in it. But honor alone will never compensate for your sacrifices in Europe, nor your sacrifices in America; a reward of another kind is due. Justice to yourself and to your friends points out the necessity of your endeavoring to procure it."

Completely tired out, Steuben, on December 5, 1782, addressed a letter to the President of Congress, asking him to appoint a committee of three to confer with him about his situation and to investigate the testimonials of the commander-in-chief as well as of other principal officers of the army in regard to his merits. It did not take the members of this committee long to become aware of the desperate situation. On Monday, December 30th, the committee reported that the sacrifices and services of Baron Steuben justly entitled him to a generous compensation, whenever the situation of public affairs would admit; that the Baron had considerable arrearages to pay due him, and that having exhausted his resources in past expenses, it was now indispensable that a sum of money should be paid him for his present support. It was proposed that the sum of $2,400 be paid him for that purpose and that he be allowed $300 per month to cover his traveling expenses during his frequent journeys. Congress adopted these propositions, and thus this matter closed for the moment. It does not appear that Steuben received any payment. And so he returned to Washington's headquarters at Newburgh.

When Steuben arrived at Washington's headquarters he found that the conditions of the army had grown from bad to worse. The officers, oppressed with debts and with the sufferings of their families at home, had in December, 1782, sent a committee to Philadelphia, to submit to Congress the following memorandum:

"We, the officers of the army of the United States, in behalf of ourselves and our brethren the soldiers, beg leave freely to state to the supreme power, our head and sovereign, the great distress under which we labor. Our embarrassments thicken so fast that many of us are unable to go farther. Shadows have been offered to us, while the substance has been gleaned by others. The citizens murmur at the greatness of their taxes, and no part reaches the army. We have borne all that men can bear. Our property is expended; our private resources are at an end. We therefore beg that a supply of money may be forwarded to the army as soon as possible. The uneasiness of the soldiers for want of pay is great and dangerous, further experiments on their patience may have fatal effects. There is a balance due for retained rations, forage, and arrearages on the score of clothing. Whenever there has been a real want of means, defect in system or in execution, we have invariably been the sufferers by hunger and nakedness, and by languishing in a hospital, etc."

The memorandum contained also the offer to commute the half pay for life, granted to the officers by the resolution of October, 1780, for half pay for a certain number of years, or for a reasonable sum in gross.

The members of the committee, chosen from among

the officers themselves, had waited in Philadelphia until the beginning of March, 1783, when they reported that nothing had been accomplished. Indignation over the failure was general. Two days after the arrival of the report, copies of an open letter were scattered broadcast through all the camps. Evidently it was written by an able person, but bore no signature.* It called upon all officers to assemble on March the 15th at the "Temple," a large frame building which had been erected as a place of worship for the army. While the letter asked the officers to decide on measures the army should take to remedy its many grievances, it was well calculated to influence the passions of the troops. Reviewing the unparalleled sufferings and hardships they had endured in many years, they were then asked questions how they had been rewarded. And then the letter burst forth:

"If this be your treatment while the swords you wear are necessary to the protection of your country, what have you to expect from peace when your voice shall sink and your strength dissipate by division, when those very swords, the instruments and companions of your glory, shall be taken from your sides, and no remaining mark of your military distinction left you but your infirmities and scars? Can you consent to retire from the field and grow old in poverty, wretchedness, and contempt? Can you consent to wade through the vile mire of dependency, and owe the remnant of that life to charity which has hitherto been spent in honor?

"If you can, go and carry with you the jest of Tories, the scorn of Whigs, and, what is worse, the pity of the world. Go, starve and be forgotten!"

Growing bold in indignation, the author attacked Washington himself, exclaiming: "Suspect the man who would advise to more moderation and longer forbearance! If you revolt at this, and would oppose tyranny under whatever garb it may assume, awake, attend to your situation, and redeem yourselves! If the present moment be lost, every future effort will be in vain, and

---
* As was afterwards discovered, this appeal was written by Major John Armstrong, an aide-de-camp of General Gates.

your threats will be empty as your entreaties are now."

The appeal closed with this direful proposition: "Tell Congress that with them rests the responsibilty of the future; that if peace returns, nothing but death shall separate you from your arms; if the war continues, you will retire to some unsettled country to smile in turn, and mock when their fear cometh!"

A copy of this letter came into the hands of Washington. What must have been his thoughts, when this ominous appeal stared him in his face?

In a splendid article, "Last Days of Washington's Army at Newburgh" (Harpers Monthly of October, 1883), the historian J. T. Headley has sketched the situation in such a masterly manner that no other attempt could surpass it.

Therefore it may be quoted here.

"A frightful gulf opened at the very feet of Washington, and he gazed with a beating heart and like one stunned into its gloomy depths. These brave men whom he had borne on his great heart these seven long years were asked to throw him overboard at last! Must it be, then, that the stormy and bloody road they had travelled together so long was to end in this awful abyss in which home and country and honor were to go down in one black ruin? As he looked on the appalling prospect his heart sank within him, and he afterward said it was "the darkest day of his life." Not in the gloomy encampment of Valley Forge, when the gazed on his half-naked, starving army dying around him, did the future look so hopeless. No lost battlefield ever bore so terrible an aspect. But what was to be done? The meeting had been called for the next day, so that there would be no time for passion to subside or cooler counsels to prevail. Should he forbid the meeting, as he had the power to do? No; the army was in no temper to submit to dictation. Besides, if he did, the evil would not be remedied. He must have something more than obedience; he must win back the love and confidence of the army, or all would be lost. He well knew that when that army once broke away from him in anger and defiance, nothing but the blackness of desolation awaited his country."

Greatly disturbed, Washington summoned his most trusted officers to consult on the proper course of action. They came one after another: Greene, Steuben, Knox, Wayne, Putnam, Sullivan and several others. It was decided, that an order should be issued at once, forbidding a meeting at the call of an anonymous paper, but directing all officers to assemble on the 18th of March, to hear the report of their committee at Philadelphia, and to determine what course should be pursued for the future. Washington was to attend the meeting and open it in person.

When the day of the meeting arrived, and the officers had assembled, Washington exhorted them on vigorous sentences to remain loyal and obedient, true to the great cause they were following, and true to their own country. Referring to the anonymous writer of the appeal, he exclaimed: "My God! what can this writer have in view in recommending such measures? Can he be a friend to our country? No! he is plotting its ruin. Let me conjure you in the name of our common country, as you value your own sacred honor, as you respect the rights of humanity, as you regard the military or natural character of America, to express your utmost horror and detestation of the man who wishes under any specious pretense to overturn our liberty, and who wickedly attempts to open the flood-gates of civil discord, and deluge our rising empire in blood."

Urging all officers as well as the men to exhibit the same patriotism and devotion to duty as before he closed his address with the words: "By thus determining and acting you will pursue the plain and direct road to the attainment of your wishes; you will defeat the insidious designs of our enemies, who are compelled to resort from open force to secret artifice; and you will give one more distinguished proof of unexampled patriotism and patient virtue, rising superior to the most complicated sufferings, and you will by the dignity of your conduct afford occasion for posterity to say, when speaking of the glorious example you have exhibited to mankind: Had this day been wanting the world had never seen the last stage of perfection to which human virtue is capable of attaining."

Withdrawing now, Washington left it to the officers to decide the actions they might feel inclined to take. Soon enough a committee called, assuring him that all who had been present, reciprocated his affectionate expressions with the greatest sincerity of which the human heart is capable."

Fortunately, on April 17th, 1783, Washington received the official information of Congress, that a treaty of peace between England and the United States had been concluded on January 20th. Freed of a load of care, the commander issued the following order:

Headquarters, Newburgh, April 18th, 1783.

"The commander-in-chief orders the cessation of hostilities between the United States of America and the King of Great Britain to be publicly read to-morrow at 12 o'clock at the new building, and the proclamation which will be communicated herewith to be read tomorrow evening at the head of every regiment and corps of the army. After which the chaplains with the several brigades will render thanks to the Allmighty God for all His mercies, particularly for His overruling the wrath of men to His own glory, and causing the rage of war to cease among the nations."

In the camps the welcome news was received with unbounded joy. The weary struggle for independence was over now, and so every soldier joined in happy mood in the preparations for a day of jubilee, at which the great event should be celebrated

Great masses of timber were cut down and carried to the lofty summits of the nearby mountains. Kindled in the evening, they blazed during the whole night "like altar fires to the God of Peace."

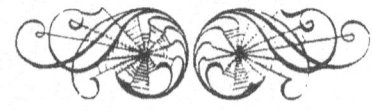

Disbanding the Revolutionary Army and the Founding of the Society of the Cincinnati.

After the grand celebration was over, the question next in order was the disbandment of the army. It fell to the lot of Steuben, to supervise this procedure, a very serious and most unpleasant one, as no money was at hand, to pay the troops their arrears, or to provide them with sufficient means for their homeward march.

On April 23, Richard Peters, chairman of the War Board, had directed a letter to Steuben (in vol. IX of the Steuben Papers) in which he confessed his inability to provide the means, necessary to pay the troops.

"Our circumstances" so he wrote "afford an odd contrast to those we have heretofore experienced. The difficulty which heretofore oppressed us was how to raise an army; the one which now embarasses us is how to dissolve it. Everything that Congress can do for our deserving soldiers will be done, but an empty purse is a bar to the execution of the best plans. We have just under consideration a plan for establishing a mint. All we want to put it in execution is the necessary metal."

An empty purse! Here the financial dilemma, the cause of so much morosity, mutiny and treason rose again, to embitter the troops even on the days of their departure.

Steuben, in response to a request by the commander-in-chief, had laid out a plan for the disbandment of the army. He suggested that the dismissal of the troops should be executed with the greatest dignity possible, that every retiring officer should receive a certificate, expressing the value of his services. Furthermore, that these certificates ought to be printed on parchment signed by the commander-in-chief, and sealed with his arms. Also every soldier, before dismissal should receive a printed testimony stating that the holder had devoted his time as well as his best services in true patriotism for the good cause of his country. This testimony should aid him as an evidence of is services and as a legal document in all further transactions of his life.

All discharges should be kept on record. Furthermore Steuben had suggested, that the troops should be discharged in line, and that all regiments or battalions should march to certain rallying points in their respective States, to be finally dismissed there by the Governor and all other authorities in a dignified manner.

Unfortunately the lack of money made it impossible to carry these suggestions out. So Congress authorized the commander-in-chief to grant furloughs as liberally as possible. Following these instructions, numerous furloughs were granted throughout spring and summer of 1783. There was no grand review of assembled regiments. The troops simply disbanded; many left by water in sloops, many on foot, single or in squads, unpaid and unrewarded except by a resolution of Congress giving them "the thanks of their country for their long, eminent and faithful service."

So the glorious army of the Revolution dwindled away. The following letter expresses Steuben's feelings during these days:

"Every man played his part in the melancholy scene according his character. As I could not trust my temper, I shut myself up in my rooms and pleaded illness. Each corps was disbanded by separate orders to the commander of each regiment, with the exception of the general order announcing the resolution of Congress. Each corps dispersed without leave-taking on either side. As Congress said nothing to either officer or soldiers, the commander-in-chief did not see fit to say anything, although everyone considered this an absolute dismissal. I was the only person who had to bear the sad farewells of the officers and soldiers. They came to visit me in my retreat, and nearly all of them in heartbroken accents began the conversation by asking me what I thought of the way they had been dismissed. Not venturing to say what I thought I had nothing left to do but assure them of my friendship, and console them as well as I could. The New York regiments, which were a model of discipline and order for the entire army, were disbanded the same day. The officers did me the honor to present me with an address. As they only addressed the Governor and myself, how do you think the proceedings will be regarded? However that may be, I feel infinitely flattered, and their kindly sentiments towards me will be the consolation of my old days."

The address, presented to Steuben on June 9th reads as follows:

"Sir! The objects for which we took upon us the profession of arms being accomplished, we are now about to retire from the field, and return to the class of private citizens. But before we separate forever, permit us, the officers of the two New York regiments, to express our feelings toward you on this occasion. The essential and distinguished services you have rendered this country must inspire the breast of every citizen of America with sentiments of gratitude and esteem. But we, Sir, feel sentiments of another nature. Your unremitted exertions on all occasions to alleviate the distress of the army, and the manner in which you have shared them with us, have given you more than a common title to the character of our friend—as our military parent we have long considered you. Ignorant as we were of the profession we had undertaken, it is to your abilities and unwearied assiduity we are indebted for that military reputation we finally attained. We therefore feel ourselves bound to you by the strongest ties of affection, and we now take leave of you with that regret which such sentiments must occasion. Wishing you long to enjoy in health and happiness those rewards which your services have merited, and which a grateful people cannot fail to bestow, we have the honor to remain, yours, etc."

It was during these melancholy times, that Steuben suggested the founding of a patriotic society* organized for the purpose of uniting all the generals and officers who had served under Washington into a union of true friendship and brotherhood. The organization meeting was held on May 13, 1783 at Steuben's headquarters in Verplanck's Mansion near Fishkill on the Hudson. Steuben acted as presiding officer. Each regiment and staff corps was represented. The constitution of the society, adopted at that day, was drafted by a committee consisting of the Generals Knox and Hand and Captain Shaw. It states that

"It having pleased the Supreme Governor of the universe in the disposition of human affairs to cause the separation of the Colonies of North America from the dominion of Great Britain and after a bloody conflict of eight years to establish them free, independent and sovereign States, cemented by alliances founded on reciprocal advantages with some of the greatest princes and powers of the earth;

"To perpetuate, therefore, as well the remembrance of this vast event as well as the mutual friendships which have been formed under the pressure of common danger, and, in many instances, cemented by the blood of the parties, the officers of the American army do hereby, in the most solemn manner, associate, constitute and combine themselves into one Society of Friends, to endure as long as they shall endure, or any of their oldest male posterity, and in failure thereof, the collateral branches, who may be judged worthy of becoming its supporters and members.

"The officers of the American army, having generally been taken from the citizens of America, possess high veneration for the character of that illustrious Roman, Lucius Quintius Cincinnatus; and being resolved to follow his example by returning to their citizenship, they think they may with propriety denominate themselves

---

*That Steuben was the real author of the society, appears from the following letter of General Heath in the "Steuben Papers" vol. X.

Newburgh, May 18, 1783.
Sir:
I have been honored with yours of this date covering the proceedings of a board of officers of the American army, and the plan of an institution for forming a society as therein is described.
If agreeable to you the plan of the institution shall be presented to his Excellency the Commander-in-Chief on Tuesday next at one o'clock p. m., and I request you will have the goodness to give General Knox the necessary notice.
I have the honor to be with great respect,
Sir, your obedient servant,
M. HEATH.

"THE SOCIETY OF THE CINCINNATI."

"The following principles shall be immutable, and form the basis of the Society of the Cincinnati: "An incessant attention to preserve inviolate those exalted rights and liberties of human nature for which they have fought and bled, and without which the high rank of rational being is a curse instead of a blessing. An unalterable determination to promote and cherish between the respective States that union and national honor so essentially necessary to the happiness and the future dignity of the American empire. To render permanent the cordial affection existing among the officers; this spirit will dictate brotherly kindness in all things, and particularly extend to the most substantial acts of beneficence, according to the ability of the society towards those officials and their families who, unfortunately, may be under the necessity of receiving it."

At the close of the organization meeting a committee, consisting of Steuben and the generals Knox and Heath waited on Washington to request him to accept the nomination as the first member as well as the president of the order. It is needless to say, that Washington, deeply moved, accepted this nomination which he appreciated as a great honor as well as a demonstration of genuine loyalty, standing in strong contrast to the acts of conspiracy and treason, he so often had to deal with.

For convenience sake the society was arranged into State societies, the general society of the order being required to meet at least once in every three years and to be composed of the general officers and a representation of not more than five delegates from each State society. All commissioned officers of the American army who had served at least three years of the war and been honorably discharged, and all commissioned officers who had been rendered supernumerary and honorably discharged in any one of the several reductions of the army, irrespective of length of service, and all commissioned officers who were actually in service at the definite peace, and until disbandment, were entitled to become original members. Subsequently, at the first meeting, held in May, 1784 in Independence Hall, Philadelphia, this was extended to include commissioned officers of State Militia or volunteers having been in the service of the United States over three years, and all Continental Naval officers of like service. Each State society was permitted to be a judge of the qualifications of its members and to elect a limited number of honorary members. Thirteen State societies were constituted in the United States and one in France. But as Congress, after the Revolution, violated its promise of half-pay for life to its officers and as nearly all were ruined in fortune, many officers had to take up their bounty lands in Kentucky, Tennessee, or Ohio, and settle there. Besides, these veterans grew older and attendance upon meetings grew more and more difficult. So several of the State societies ceased to exist, and for some years no general meetings were held.

With the revival of the interest in patriotic organizations that began with the centennial celebrations in 1875, successful efforts were made to reorganize the dormant State societies of the Cincinnati, so that at the present time there are again societies in each of the original thirteen States. These State societies annually meet on July 4, and afterwards the members dine together, with customary toasts suitable to the day.

The ensignia of the society was designed by Major L'Enfant, the same, who later on became famous as the designer of the plans for the city of Washington. The emblem of the order consists of a golden eagle, bearing on the breast a medallion showing the Roman Cincinnatus accepting a sword from three Roman Senators. In the background his wife is leaning at the door of his home, and also a plow and other agricultural implements are shown. This medallion has the inscription "Omnia relinquit Servare Rempublicam." "He left everything behind to serve the republic." On the reverse side of the emblem the goddess Fame is seen crowning Cincinnatus with a wreath of laurels. It bears the inscription "Virtutis Praemium," "The Reward of Virtue." In the background a maritime city is shown with vessels entering the harbor. Below this are clasped hands supporting a heart inscribed "Esto Perpetua," "Be thou Forever." Around the whole are the words: "Societas Cincinnatorum Instituta A. D. 1783." This insignia is attached to a blue ribbon edged with white.—

When the terms of peace had been received Washington brought to the attention of Congress the importance of getting immediate possession of these frontier posts, which according to the peace treaty were within the boundaries of the United States, but were still held by the British. He succeeded in having Steuben sent out as a special commissioner to obtain the surrender of these forts, to exchange guns and other stores, and to inspect, in what direction these forts might be improved. Steuben set out in July arriving at Chamblee on the Sorel river on August 24. But here he found to his great dismay that his mission, as he had feared, was in vain. General Haldimand, the British commander of the frontier posts, informed him that his government so far had given him no instructions for the evacuation of the posts, that he had only received orders to cease hostilities, and that he therefore could not turn over an inch of ground until he should receive positive orders for that purpose. For the same reasons it would be impossible for him to permit Steuben to visit a single post occupied by the British. As the generals position was technically correct, nothing remained to Steuben but to return. In fact, the question of these posts was not settled for many years. The British, pretending that the Americans had not lived up to the stipulations of the treaty, and that such citizens, as had remained loyal to King George during the war, had been treated unfairly, held the posts until 1796, thus causing to the Americans many troubles.

After his return from this errant, Steuben went to Philadelphia, to finish up military business. He remained here for some time, but he was again with Washington's staff, when, on the morning of November 3, the last detachments of the glorious Revolutionary army broke ranks. It was a sad parting. A band played the mournful strains of "Roslyn Castle" which had been always played when a dead comrade was carried to his grave. Then came an act, of which Dr. Thatcher, who was present, said that it was painful beyond description. "Both officers and soldiers, long unaccustomed to the affairs of private life, were turned loose upon the world. Never can the day be forgotten when friends and companions for seven years in joy and sorrow were torn assunder without the hope of even meeting again, and with the prospect of a miserable subsistance in the future."

Major North, another witness of the scene, gave the following account in his notes:

"The inmates of the same tent for seven long years grasped each other's hands in silent agony, to go they knew not whither; all recollections of the art to thrive by civil service lost, or to the youthful never known, their hard-earned military knowledge worse than useless, and to be cast out into the world by them long since forgotten; to go in silence and alone, and poor and helpless. Oh, on that sad day how many hearts were wrung! I saw it all, nor will the scene be ever blotted from my view."

North also states, that "the kind-hearted Steuben looked on the scene with pitying eyes. Seeing Colonel Cochrane, a brave, gallant officer, standing apart and leaning on his sword while his face expressed the deepest sadness, Steuben approached him and said "Cheer up; better times are coming!"

"For myself," replied the officer, "I can stand it; but" pointing to a mere hovel near by, he added "my wife and daughters are in that wretched tavern. I have nowhere to carry them, nor even money to remove them."

"Come, come" said the Baron, "I will pay my respects to Mrs. Cochrane and your daughters," and leaving him standing alone, he strode away to the tavern, where he found the ladies sunk in despondency. The sight was too much for the brave veteran, and emptying his purse on the table, he hastened away to escape their tears and their blessings."

North relates another incident. "A black man, with wounds not yet healed, wept on the wharf; for it was at Newburgh where these sad scenes were passing. There was a vessel in the stream bound to the place where this poor soldier once had friends; he could not pay his passage. Where found or borrowed I know not, but the Baron soon returned. The man hailed the sloop, and cried: "God bless you Massa Baron; God Almighty bless you!" But why do I relate these scraps of benevolence, when all who knew him and were worthy, knew him as their friend? What good or honorable man, civil or military, before the parting times which sundered friendships, did not respect and love the Baron? Who most? Those who knew him best."—

After the departure of the last troops Washington, accompanied by his staff and body guard, went to New York, to take possession of that city, which was evacuated by the British on November 25.

Having everything accomplished now, Washington prepared to go to Annapolis, to offer his resignation to Congress, which was there in session. But before his departure he once more assembled his generals on December 5th in Fraunce's Tavern for a farewell dinner.

Colonel Benjamin Tallmadge, who was among those present, has in his memoirs related this affair as follows: "We had been assembled but a few moments, when his Excellency entered the room. His emotion, too strong to be concealed, seemed to be reciprocated by every officer present. After partaking of a slight refreshment in almost breathless silence, the General filled his glass with wine, and turning to the officers, said "With a heart full of love and gratitude I now take leave of you, wishing most devoutly that your latter days may be as prosperous and happy as your former ones have been glorious and honorable."

After the officers had taken a glass of wine, the general added: "I can not come to each of you, but shall feel obliged if each of you will come and take me by the hand!" General Knox, being nearest to him, turned to the commander-in-chief, who, suffused in tears, was incapable of utterance, but grasped his hand, when they embraced each other in silence. In the same affectionate manner every officer in the room marched up, kissed, and parted with his General-in-chief. Such a scene of sorrow and wheeping I had never before witnessed, and hope I may never be called upon to witness again. Not a word was uttered to break the solemn silence that prevailed, or to interrupt the tenderness of the interesting scene. The simple thought that we were about to part from the man who had conducted us through a long and bloody war, and under whose conduct the glory and independence of our country had been achieved, and that we should see his face no more in this world seemed to me utterly insupportable. But the time of separation had come, and waving his hand to his grieving children around him, he left the room, and walked silently on to Whitehall, where a barge was in waiting. We all followed in mournful silence to the wharf, where a prodigious crowd had assembled to witness the departure of the man, who, under God, had been the great agent in establishing the glory and independence of these United States. As soon as he was seated, the barge put off into the river, and when out in the stream, our great and beloved general waved his hat, and bade us a silent farewell."

Having stopped at Philadelphia for a few days, Washington arrived at Annapolis on December 20th, addressing at the same day a letter to Congress, asking when it would be agreeable to them to receive him. Arrangements were made for noon of December 23rd. But before he went to tender his resignation, he penned the following noble letter* to the most faithful of his comrades in arms, to Baron von Steuben:

Annapolis, decr. 23d 1783.

"My dear Baron:

Altho' I have taken frequent Opportunities both in public and private, of Acknowledging your great Zeal, Attention and Abilities in performing the duties of your Office: yet, I wish, to make use of this last Moment of my public life to Signify in the strongest terms, my entire Approbation of your Conduct, and to express my

Sense of the Obligations the public is under to you for your faithful, and Meritorious Services.

I beg you will be convinced, my dear Sir, that I should rejoice, if it could ever be in my power, to serve you more essentially, than by expressions of regard and Affection—but in the mean time, I am persuaded you will not be displeased with this farewell token of my Sincere Friendship and Esteem for you.

This, is the last letter I shall ever write, while I continue in the Service of my Country—the hour of my Resignation is fixed at twelve this day—after which I shall become a private Citizen on the Banks of the Potomack, where I shall be glad to embrace you, and testify the great Esteem and Consideration, with which

I am My Dear Baron
Your most Obedt. and Affectn.

Go. Washington.

The Honble
Major Genl. Baron de Steuben

To this document, full of expressions of gratitude, Steuben gave the following reply**

"My Dear General

The letter of December 23d which I have had the honor of receiving from Your Excellency, is the most honorable testimony which my services could have received. My first wish was to approve myself to Your Excellency, & in having obtained it, my happiness is complete.

The Confidence Your Excellency was pleased to place in my integrity & ability gained me that of the army & of the United States, Your approbation will secure it.

A stranger to the language and customs of the Country, I had nothing to offer in my favor but a little experience & great good will to serve the United States;

---

* Washington's Writings, vol. VIII. 503.
** A copy of this letter is in Vol. X of the "Steuben Papers" in the New York Historical Society.

If my endeavors have succeeded I owe it to Your Excellency's protection & it is a sufficient reward for me to know that I have been useful in Your Excellency's Operations which always tended to the good of Your country.

After having studied the principles of the military art under Frederick, & put them in practice under Washington, after having deposited my sword under the same trophies of Victory with yours, & finally after having received this last public testimony of your esteem, there remains nothing for me to desire.

Accept my sincere thanks, My dear General for the unequivocal proofs of your friendship which I have received since I had first the honor to receive your orders; & believe that I join my prayers to those of America for the preservation of your life, & for the increase of your felicity. With every sentiment of respect, I have the honor to be
Your Excellency's Obedient

Steuben."

A few words may be added about Washington's body guard. As there was no longer need to protect him against enemies, this guard too was dissolved. Only eleven men, including Colonel Meytinger, a sergeant and a trumpeter were retained to escort under command of Major von Heer Washington to his home Mount Vernon in Virginia. Having arrived there the faithful soldiers once more lined up in front of the manor house for a last parade. Once more words of command were given, once more the glittering swords were drawn in saluting, then the brave men rode quietly away, with heavy hearts, that they had to depart from their beloved chief, whom they for many years had protected in all his sorrows and cares.

The last member of this guard, Ludwig Boyer, died in 1843 on his farm in Miami County, Ohio, 87 years old.

The whole number of regular troops or "Continentals," employed during the Revolutionary War, was 231,791. Of these Massachusetts furnished 67,907, Connecticut 31,939; Virginia 26,678; Pennsylvania 25,678, and the other States smaller numbers, down to 2,679 from Georgia. The expenditures of the contest, as officially estimated in 1790, were in specie $92,485,693, and the debts, foreign expenditures, etc., swelled this to $135,693,703.

Years of Disappointments and Blighted Hopes.

When the question of the disbandment of the army was discussed in Congress, it appeared that a number of troops must be retained in service in order to guard the military stores established at various points of the country as well as to protect the settlers at the western frontier against the frequent raids by hostile Indians. These considerations caused a lively discussion of the question whether the United States should have a standing army of regular troops.

Many delegates were strongly opposed to such an institution, as they had a deep aversion to any form of soldiery. Especially the delegates from the New England States were unanimously in favor of a resolution declaring that "standing armies in times of peace are inconsistent with the principles of republican government, as they are dangerous to the liberties of a free people, and generally converted into destructive engines for establishing despotism."

Steuben, well aware that the future might bring again serious quarrels with England or other European countries, emphasized that it would be wise to prepare in times of peace for war, and that every citizen ought to be well trained in the use of arms and ready for the defense of his country. He therefore proposed the formation of a regular army, to consist of 21,000 established militia men, 3,000 federal troops, and 1,000 artillerists and pioneers. This plan was approved by Washington, and later on adopted by Congress. The strength of this standing army, as suggested by Steuben, remained the same until the outbreak of the Civil War.

To provide this army with able commanders and officers, Steuben suggested the founding of a regular Military Academy, where young men, having the intention to devote themselves to a military career, might obtain a perfect physical training as well as the very best and most liberal education in military sciences, history, geography, civil law and the law of nations, fencing, dancing, music, etc. At the request of the Secretary of War, General Benjamin Lincoln, Steuben submitted detailed plans for such an academy* and proposed that its faculty should have a director general, four senior officers and two professors with a number of other instructors; furthermore, that the Academy should have 120 cadets, 80 of whom destined for infantry officers, 20 for cavalry, and 20 for artillery and engineers. A manufacturing establishment, connected with the academy, was to provide everything necessary for the use of the army. To prevent future appointments to commanding positions in the army of inexpert persons, Steuben suggested that Congress should pass a law by which no person should be employed as an officer in the army, who had not served as an officer in the late war, or received his education at the military academy.

Washington argued for years in favor of Steuben's plans, but no action was taken until March 16, 1802, when by an act of Congress the Military Academy at West Point was established which has given to the army of the United States so many able commanders.

To the deep regret of all patriotic Americans Steuben's service soon afterwards came to an end.

When in 1784 General Benjamin Lincoln resigned

---

* Volume X of the "Steuben Papers" contains the following letter of Lincoln to Steuben:

War Office, April 24, 1783.

"Dear Baron!

"I have been honored with your favor of the 16th inst. covering a system for the Military Academy.

"I am exceedingly obliged by your attention to this subject and for your well digested and judicious arrangements; please do accept my most cordial thanks.

"I am fully convinced what is the interest of the United States, but cannot be so certain what line of conduct they will pursue, however the Committee have under consideration your observations. If I differ from them in my report it will not be because I think them not well calculated to promote the general interest but from a full conviction that so necessary and extensive a plan cannot be carried in Congress. I hope you will be heard before your plan shall be rejected. If the very best measure cannot be obtained we must at present content with the next.

Lincoln."

111

as Secretary of War, Steuben applied for this position, convinced that he could render still greater services to the country of his adoption. But his aspirations were frustrated by a clique of political wire-pullers, who were eager to secure that office for General Henry Knox, who was much younger than Steuben. For want of a better pretext these tricky ring-leaders explained, that the office of the Secretary of War was far too important a one to be intrusted to a "foreigner", because such a person might in time of war betray the country to the enemy.

When on this flimsy plea the position was given to Knox, Steuben regarded this action as a reflection on his honor, as an expression of distrust in his often proven devotion to the interests of the republic. And had not the State of Pennsylvania by a special act of the Legislature in March, 1783 made him a full fledged citizen of that commonwealth? Was he, in spite of this act, still a "foreigner"? Certainly he was justified in expressing his indignation in the following caustic remarks:

"The man who had abandoned all his appointments and the brightest prospects in Europe, to devote his services to the United States, who had served them with zeal and fidelity during the war of seven years as critical as trying; the man who had got possessions in Virginia, Pennsylvania, New York and New Jersey,—with what effrontery could he be called a foreigner? As to the importance of this ministerial office, the man who organized the whole American army in the midst of the war; the man who solely had established and put in execution the principles of strict military rules: this man cannot be intrusted with the administration of a corps of four hundred men in time of peace! What fine reasoning! But, in fact, Mr. Knox had engaged the delegates of Massachusetts to secure to him this place. His own State could not provide him with a post worthy of his ambition, and therefore the Confederacy had to give him a suitable appointment. Without disputing his knowledge in the use of artillery, I dare assert that on my arrival at the army, it had no idea of maneuvering with a single field piece, and that I was the first who taught them to make use of their cannon in the attack and retreat."

On March 24, 1784, Steuben presented his resignation to the President of Congress with the following letter:

"Sir:
"Tho a foreigner, I flatter myself that my zeal for the interests of the United States renders me worthy to participate in the happiness of seeing this Confederacy exalted to that Rank which the Virtue and perseverance of its Citizens have merited.

"The object for which I left my country, my friends & all that was dear to me, is accomplished.—My companions in the late war have returned to the Class of Citizens, rewarded by the success which has attended their patriotic labours. The French Officers satisfied with the honorary & pecuniary rewards they have received from the United States, still expect from the bounty of their Sovereign those marks of his approbation which he waits to bestow.—My feelings inform me that it is time to quit the stage & to sheath that sword which has ben drawn (for the last time) in this glorious revolution.

"I Return into the hands of Congress the Commission which I had the honor to receive from that honorable Body, & beg they will accept my respectful acknowledgements for the confidence with which I have been honored."

Congress accepted this resignation on April 15, with the following resolution:

"Resolved, That the thanks of the United States, in Congress assembled, be given to Baron Steuben for the great zeal and abilities he has discovered in the discharge of the several duties of his office; that a gold-hilted sword be presented to him as a mark of the high sense Congress entertain of his character and services, and that the superintendent of finance take order for procuring the same."

The sword mentioned in the above resolution was forwarded to Steuben almost three years later with the following letter from General Knox, the Secretary of War:

War Office, Jan. 4, 1787.

"Sir,

The United States in Congress assembled by their act of the 15th of April 1784 expressed their high sense of your military talents, services, and character, and as an honorable evidence thereof, they directed that a gold hilted sword should be presented to you. It is with great satisfaction I embrace the occasion of presenting you with the invaluable memorial of their sentiments and your eminent merits.

Were it possible to enhance the honor conferred by the sovereign authority, it would be derived from the consideration, that their applause was reciprocated by the late illustrious commander in chief, and the whole Army.

I have the honor to be, Sir, With the most perfect consideration,

Your obedient and humble servt.

H. Knox."

To this letter Steuben replied on January 5, 1787, as follows:
"Sir,

I have been honored with your letter, and Capt. Stagg has delivered me the sword which the United States were pleased to order by their act of the 15th of April 1784.

Permit me, sir, to request that you express to Congress the high sentiments of respect and acknowledgement with which I received this distinguished mark of their regard.

To a soldier such sentiments are ever dear, and that this is accompanied with the approbation of our late commander in chief, of yourself, and the army in general, will always be my greatest glory.

Accept sir, my sincere thanks for the very flattering

manner in which you have communicated this present, and believe me Sir, &c.

Steuben."

A description of the sword was published in the New York Daily Advertiser of January 11, 1787. "It was made in London under the direction of Col. Smith, and executed by the first workmen in that kingdom. The small medallions on each side of the top of the hilt present an eagle perched on a bunch of arrows, with a wreath of laurel in her bill and wings extended ready to rise. The modest Genius of America fills the front medallion on the hilt, dressed in a flowing robe, ornamented with the new constellation, holding an olive branch in her right arm, and a dagger in her left hand, and the fair field of liberty flourishing in the background. It is answered on the opposite side with the full figure of Minerva, in martial dress, robed and ornamented with the same stars; the bird of wisdom is seated near; her left hand being extended, presents the olive branch, while the right is properly supported by the spear, this figure is martial and gay; the other is mild and modestly embraces the olive branch, but holds the dagger with firmness. The bow of the hilt presents drums, colours, halberts, etc. etc. etc. The sword and blue book fills the two lower ones,—two eagles, seated on knots of colours, surrounded with stars and holding a sprig of an olive branch in the bill with extended wings, are emblems of peace and protection, under the sword and blue book. The two opposite medallions are filled with trophies of war, and the following inscription modestly placed out of view, under the shield: "The United States to Major General Baron Steuben, 15th, April, 1784, for military merit."

Steuben, in his last will bequeathed this sword to his aide-de-camp Major Benjamin Walker. Efforts made a number of years ago to locate this sword have not been successful.

* * *

At the time, when Congress accepted Steuben's resignation, his total claims due him for his work and the financial obligations he had incurred, amounted to $50,000. Congress resolved that the proper officers should proceed with the liquidation of this money in the most speedy and efficacious manner. But Congress was in such a state, that its resolutions and promises had no value at all.

McMaster in an article on Washington's inauguration (Harper's Monthly April 1889) hardly overdrew the picture.

"Acting on the States and not on the people, Congress never won the affections of the people, but was looked on, was spoken of, was treated as a foreign government rather than a creature of their own making. When a band of ploughmen gathered under the window of its room at Philadelphia and broke up its sitting with taunts and threats, not a citizen could be found willing to aid in defending it. Driven from the city, it fled to Princeton, and there found a refuge under the guns of fifteen hundred soldiers. From Princeton it soon adjourned to Annapolis. There, disgusted at the perpetual sitting of Congress, the Rhode Island delegates, acting under instructions from their Legislature, moved a recess. This was carried, and, as the Articles of Confederation required, a committee of the States was chosen to sit during the recess. But the members quarelled, separated with bitter words, and for two months the country was without a general government of any kind. In November, 1784, the Congress reassembled at Trenton, and from Trenton in time they adjourned to New York. In the taverns, meanwhile, the wits were expressing their contempt in the popular toasts "A hoop for the barrel!" "Cement for the Union!" In the newspapers Congress was likened to a wheel rolling from Dan to Beersheba and from Beersheba to Dan. Neglected by its members, insulted by the troops, a wanderer from town to town, the subject of jest by the people, the Congress of the Confederation sank rapidly to the condition of a debating club. It made requisitions that never were heeded, voted monuments that never were put up, rewarded great men with sums of money that never were paid, planned wise schemes for the payment of the debt that never were carried out, and looked on in helplessness while English troops held and fortified American forts."

Now, what could be expected of such a council that had no permanent headquarters and whose membership was changing from year to year? The Congress at Annapolis, which accepted Steuben's resignation, was composed of entirely different men from those who had been present in 1778 at York, when Steuben made his noble offer to the United States. Besides, many of these new members were ordinary human beings, not open to noble feelings, but moved by personal interests, and always apt to consider local claims rather than military merits. There were other obstacles. The "records"—if such designation can be used for the few incoherent notes made by the secretaries of Congress—contained nothing about the contract, the special committee had made with Steuben in 1778 at York. And so the majority of the new Congressmen, totally ignorant of Steuben's great services, were inclined to regard him as "one of those foreign adventurers who had come to America to seek fortunes."

The story of Steuben's treatment by Congress during the years 1784 to 1790 is too disgusting and tedious for detailed description. To satisfy the ignorant, Steuben was compelled to prove the existence of the contract, concluded at York, by securing certificates from those three gentlemen, who in 1778 had made the arrangements with him. These certificates, together with other papers and testimonials, were submitted to John Jay, Alexander Hamilton, James Duane, Chancellor Livingston and Duer, the leading jurists in the country, who unanimously declared the existence of a binding contract between Steuben and the Government. But in spite of this Congress left the matter undecided, referring it from one Committee to another and relaying it from year to year. Meantime, the situation of Steuben became so grave, that he had only "to chose between starving here and begging in Europe." So General J. Armstrong stated in a letter on May 30, 1788, to General Gates.

During these years Steuben was living in a suburban house of New York with his former aides-de-camp, William North and B. Walker.

Fortunately, in November, 1788, the old Continental Congress of the Confederation that had given so little satisfaction, dissolved. In September of that year only six, in October only two States were represented by delegates. "These came in day after day, sometimes six, sometimes two, would saunter into the hall, have the secretary take down their names, and then go off to their favorite tavern. But no sittings were held, no business was done, and so the Congress, whose name is bound up with so much that is glorious in the annals of our country expired ignominiously for want of a quorum."

Not before March 4, 1789 and after much quareling, a new Congress, the First Congress under the Constitution, assembled in the City Hall at New York. But it seemed to have inherited all the sloth, all the indifference and torpor of the old. The claim of Steuben was not taken up before April 6, 1790, and it was not before May 7th, after John Page of Virginia had addressed the house, that real action was taken. Disgusted by the undignified manner in which Steuben's claim had been handled so far Page rose and made the following address:

"Mr. Speaker:

"This illustrious veteran offered his services on such generous terms, and served us so essentially, that I shall blush for Congress should the ideas of some gentlemen now prevail. It is unworthy of Congress, after having so long enjoyed the benefits of those services, now to be thus coldly scrutinizing the terms on which he offered them, and speaking of them as of little importance. I shall weigh them not with the dollars proposed; they are far beyond any sum which we can give. If I should be at liberty to propose a compensation for the sacrifices he made by coming to America, and serving in her war, and to recompense him for his great services, I am sure I shall propose a much larger sum than has yet been talked of.

"Sir, had the Baron stipulated to receive but two per cent on the articles under his direction, or I may say on what he saved, he would be entitled to much more than is now proposed to be given him. The economy he introduced into the army was the occasion of an immense saving. Who can say now what was saved in arms, accoutrements, and ammunition, and by the reduction of baggage and forage? I have been told that officers, who had loaded a wagon with their baggage, were soon reduced to a single pack-horse.

"Some gentlemen have made light of the discipline which has been attributed to the Baron, and told us of the affairs of Bunker's Hill, Trenton, Princeton, and Germantown. It was true these were brilliant actions; but the member from South Carolina and the member from Delaware had replied fully to this observation. They well observed, that brilliant as those actions were, valor without discipline is often vain, and many lead only to destruction; that the commander in chief did wonders without the Baron, and he was wonderful in resources, and 'in himself a host.' But we should not now consider what the commander in chief did before he had the Baron's assistance, but what he did with his assistance, and what use he made of his services; and to this, as far as relates to the Baron, he has repeatedly and generously borne ample testimony.

"Sir, the Baron, as Adjutant-General and Director-General, was peculiarly adapted to the purpose of the American Army. Having served twenty-two years in the Prussian army, which Americans had been taught to believe was the best disciplined in the world, his discipline was more readily embraced, and more confidence reposed in it than would have been the case had almost any other man, of any other nation, undertaken that great task. The praise now given to the Baron is no disparagement therefore to other officers. The Commander-in-chief stood in need of an Adjutant like him, from the peculiar situation of our army, and has acknowledged his services; therefore it does not become us to speak of them as unimportant.

"Sir, I have asked officers, and some of them now in

this House, whether I have misunderstood or overrated the Baron's claim, and I have been constantly told that I did not. Though I had not the honor of being in the army, I was well informed by my correspondents there of many important circumstances; and on inquiring what were the effects produced by the new Adjutant and Director-General (the Baron Steuben), I was told that they were visible in many economical arrangements, in dispositions of corps, in maneuvering, in marches, in encampments, and particularly in more silent and rapid movements and preparations for action. I was told that when the Marquis de Lafayette, with a detachment under is command, was in danger of being cut off on his return to the army, and the Commander-in-chief was determined to support that invaluable officer, the whole army was under arms and ready to march in less than fifteen minutes from the time the signal was given.

"Sir, the effect of this discipline was seen in the marches of our army; they passed rivers in less time than the best troops in Europe could. Those excellent French troops, which served with them in the campaign of 1781, were inferior to them in this respect. The superiority of our troops, as to rapidity of movement, was seen in the attacks on the two redoubts of Yorktown, in Virginia.

"We have been asked, what will our officers say to this vote in favor of the Baron? I will venture to say, Sir, they will be pleased with it. They acknowledge the obligations they were under to that great man; they view his circumstances in the same light as that gallant officer does, who is now the Secretary, and who drew the report on which the bill before you is founded, and which does honor to is heart."

After this speech the discussion of the matter dragged on through the rest of April until May 10th. The original bill had provided for the pay and other emoluments of the major-general from March 10, 1778 to April 15, 1784, an annuity for life of $2,706, to commence October 1, 1777, and the grant of several thousand acres of land in the Western Territory of the United States.

On May 10th the annuity was cut down to $2,000, leaving out everything else. The Senate on May 27th increased this annuity to $2,500, and so, at last, on June 7th, the following act was adopted:

"Be it enacted by the Senate and House of Representatives of the United States of America, in Congress assembled, That, in order to make full and adequate compensation to Frederick William de Steuben, for the sacrifices and eminent services made and rendered to the United States during the late war, there be paid to the said Frederick William de Steuben an annuity of two thousand five hundred dollars, during life, to commence on the first day of January last; to be paid in quarterly payments, at the treasury of the United States; which said annuity shall be considered in full discharge of all claims and demands whatever, of the said Frederick William de Steuben against the United States.

(Signed)
FREDERICK AUGUSTUS MUHLENBERG,
Speaker of the House of Representatives.
JOHN ADAMS,
Vice-President of the United States and President of the Senate.
Approved, June 4, 1790.
G. WASHINGTON.
President of the United States."

Washington expressed his satisfaction over this act in the following words: "I rejoice that Congress has given to so excellent a patriot an independence by an annuity, for had they bestowed a specific sum, were it ten times the amount, the generous heart of Steuben would keep him poor, and he would, in all probability, die a beggar."

Cincinnatus Redivivus.

Several years before the First Congress did justice to the claim of Steuben, the legislatures of four States remembered the great services he had accomplished within their boundaries. As these States had no money to spare, they tried to express their gratitude by conferring on Steuben the privilege of citizenship and by making him considerable grants of land. Pennsylvania in March, 1783 donated 2,000 acres in the County of Westmoreland; Virginia offered 15,000 acres in the territory northwest of the Ohio; New York in May, 1786, granted him 6,000 acres north of the Mohawk river; and New Jersey testified its gratefulness by granting a life lease of an estate in Bergen County, that was to be confiscated from an alleged Tory. The gift last mentioned Steuben refused to accept, as it was against his nature to assent to the expulsion of the owner in whose behalf he interceded. While thus the States indicated their good will toward Steuben, his straightened financial conditions did not permit him to improve these virgin lands or settle them with immigrants. And so, while he was rich in landed property, he was unable to make use of it or to borrow a dollar on it.

The situation became more favorable, after Congress, on June 7, 1790, had granted Steuben an annuity. Three days later Steuben was en route to visit the tract of land, the Legislature of New York had conferred on him. As stated before, it was situated north of the Mohawk river in Oneida County. In those days, when traveling conditions were very poor, the entire journey had to be made on horse-back and took twelve days.

Arrived on the spot, Steuben found that his estate occupied a long ridge 2,000 feet high and affording an impressive view over a vast part of central and northern New York. Toward the west a large section of the

Oneida lake could be seen. As during primitive times the whole country had been covered with enormous glaciers, the character of the land was stony. Boulders of every size and shape dotted the ground, thus making it more adapted to grazing than the raising of grain.

There were already a few settlers living here, the number of which Steuben tried to increase by offering to former soldiers a present of forty to one hundred acres of land. For his own use he had a simple log cabin erected, with several rooms and a kitchen.

Here Steuben lived during the summer months of 1790 to 1794, spending his time in scientific studies and in making plans for the improvement of his property. The evening hours were devoted to the reading of good books and to the playing of chess.

For the winter Steuben returned to New York, where his days were occupied by many functions of social and public character. Not only was he President of the New York chapter of the "Society of the Cincinnati," the most vigorous of all the State organizations, but he also was elected President of the "German Society of New York."

The origin of this philanthropic institution is closely connected with the founding of the "German Society of Pennsylvania," which was started on Christmas Day of 1764, in order to fight the horrible abuses which had arisen with European immigration. English and Dutch shippers, not supervised by the authorities, who took no interest in the proper treatment and future of emigrants, had committed the most abominable crimes against these poor people. Pretending to be willing to help all persons without means, they offered such people credit for their passage across the ocean, on condition that they should earn it after their arrival in America by hiring out for a certain length of time as servants to such people who would pay their wages in advance by refunding the passage money to the shipowners. As these persons were redeeming themselves by performing this service, they were called "Redemptioners."

With this harmless-looking decoy many thousands of poor human beings were lured to sign contracts, only to find out later that they had become victims of villainous scoundrels and had to pay for their inexperience with the best years of their lives.

The abuses of this system grew in time to such an extent that the redemptioners were in fact not better treated than slaves and were often literally worked to death, to say nothing of receiving insufficient food, scanty clothing and poor lodging. Of the right to punish redemptioners, many heartless people made such frequent and cruel use, that laws became necessary whereby it was forbidden to apply to such servants more than ten lashes for each fault. Female redemptioners were quite often by all kinds of devilish tricks forced to lives of shame, conditions which some of the peculiar laws of the colonies even invited.

Incidents of such character had stirred the German citizens of Philadelphia to revolt against such infamous treatment of immigrants. Forming the "German Society of Pennsylvania" they secured in time laws by which ship-owners as well as the captains and other officials became subjected to strict control, and so many of the worst abuses were successfully stopped.

The "German Society of Pennsylvania" became the model for many similar institutions in other parts of America. The "German Society of New York," organized on August 23, 1784, grew to be the most important of all, when New York became the principal port in the United States. Steuben held the position of President of this society during the rest of his life.

In April, 1787 the Legislature of the State of New York elected Steuben one of the regents of the State University. In this capacity he had to inspect all the colleges within the state, as well as their system of education and discipline.

When Steuben assumed these various offices, his deep interest in the public life of his time is evident. In politics he also showed a great activity. It is needless to say that he was a member of the Federal Party, a firm believer in the sentence: "In Union is strength!" During the war he had constantly suffered under the many evils and unsettled conditions caused by the looseness of the Union under the Articles of Confederation. Accordingly, he was a most ardent advocate of a stronger government. Moreover, he was convinced that thus only could the Americans become a nation among nations. In various pamphlets Steuben expressed his views on these questions as well as on State and National debts, the rights and authority of the President, etc. And when his friend and former commander-in-chief, George Washington was chosen to be the first President of the United States, no one was happier than Steuben.

Washington's arrival in New York brought to Steuben once more days of honor and military splendor. He was a member of the committee that on April 23rd welcomed Washington in New York.

With Adams, Livingston, Sherman, Clinton, Knox, Otis and St. Clair Steuben stood near Washington when he, on the 30th of April 1789, on the balcony of the City Hall solemnly delivered the oath to execute faithfully his high office. He also attended the grand ball given in honor of the President on the evening of May 5, in the City Assembly Rooms, a brilliant affair, at which three hundred dignitaries, the most prominent men and the most beautiful ladies of the country were present.

During the President's and Mrs. Washington's stay in New York Steuben was one of their favorite guests at receptions and other social affairs, because for his splendid character and refined manners the "Baron"— under this title he was known in New York— was beloved by all. Nature had endowed him with a great, generous heart. And for his playful wit and esprit he was welcomed everywhere.

Former biographers of Steuben relate an incident, that occurred when some day the Baron was introduced to an exceptional beautiful young lady named Sheaf. "I am very happy indeed," said Steuben on hearing the lady's name, "in the honor of being presented to you, Mademoiselle, though I see it is at an infinite risk. I have from my youth been warned to guard myself against mis-chief, but I had no idea that her charms are so irresistible!"

While Steuben never was married, and while it is not known that he ever was in love with a lady, there have been few men, who in like measure enjoyed the esteem and friendship of nobleminded representatives of their own sex. Above all, there was Washington, followed by a long line of Generals, officers and soldiers, who during the years of war came in intimate contact with Steuben. Those who peruse the still existing letters of Major Wm. North, and Col. Benjamin Walker, the former aides-de-camp of Steuben, or the notes of his secretary J. W. Mulligan, or the many friendly communications of prominent men, must envy Steuben for having been the object of such genuine confraternity and arduous love.

The year 1794 opened with prospects that seemed to promise another chapter to Steuben's military career. England, in complete disregard of the stipulations of the treaty of peace that had been concluded ten years ago, was still holding the military posts in the northwest, among them Oswego, Detroit and Mackinac. Frictions were frequent; in time the relations between the United States and England became so strained that another war seemed imminent. In New York indignation was so intense that the Legislature began to prepare for the coming conflict by appointing a defense-commission, with orders to fortify not only New York harbor, but also several points of strategic value in the Northwest. Steuben was placed at the head of this commission, which began immediately to repair the existing fortifications and to construct new ones where necessary.

In fulfilment of this commission Steuben made a survey of the "Narrows" the southern entrance to the bay of New York, as well as of the upper parts of the East river, the Hell Gate. At the same time the fortifications on Governor's island were repaired, a work in which all members of the German Society of New York joined. On the morning of June 5th they marched, with Steuben at the head of the procession, and with flying banners and music down Broadway to the Battery, then crossing to the island to do their share in the common work.

A few days afterwards Steuben, in company with several members of the defense commission started for a journey to the northwestern parts of the state, especially the country around the Oneida and Onondaga lakes. Here friendly Indians warned Steuben, that the British commander at Fort Oswego was aware of his party, and that several hundred Canadian Indians had been sent out to capture and deliver him to the fort. As such a malicious act would at once cause the outbreak of the war, Steuben, not wishing to bring on such a calamity, abandoned further reconnoitering, hoping that the negotiations of Chief-Justice John Jay, who had been appointed minister extraordinary to Great Britain, would lead to a peaceful settlement of the question.

Steuben's Death and Last Resting Place.

During the fall Steuben was once more at his log-cabin in Oneida County. Two servants and John Mulligan, his secretary, a fine, well educated young man, were with him. Apparently Steuben was in good health. But on the morning of November 25th he suffered an apoplectic attack and at 12.30 noon on the 28th he passed away.

A still existing letter, written by Mulligan on November 29th, to Colonel Walker, tells the story of Steuben's death. Giving at the same time evidence of Mulligan's deep devotion toward his master, it may find here a place.

"I am sufficiently composed to begin, O my dear Sir, a sad tale. On Tuesday morning last our friend, my father, was struck with palsy which deprived his left side of motion. The evening before we parted at eleven; he was well, perfectly well. At four o'clock I was alarmed with the cry that he was dying, and when I entered his chamber he was in extreme agony, and appeared to have suffered long. I sent for immediate assistance, and dispatched White (one of the two servants) for Major North. He was sensible and could speak. . . . Every measure which the situation afforded was pursued to relieve him until the arrival of the doctor on Thursday. He administered medicines which gave some relief, but it was not long. The stroke was too violent, and yesterday at half past twelve o'clock, o my good God, my parent died! O, Colonel Walker, our friend, my all; I can write no more. Come if you can, I am lonely. Oh, good God, what solitude is in my bosom. Oh, if you were here to mingle your tears with mine, there would be some consolation for the distressed!"

Major North, who was at his residence in Duanesburg, near Schenectady, arrived at the log-cabin Saturday, November 29th, just in time to take part in the few preparations for the funeral. According to a desire Steuben had expressed during his life, his body was wrapped in the same military cloak that had protected him during so many years. The order of fidelity was placed on his breast, and so he was buried in the forest that surrounded his home under an old hemlock under which he sat many times and which he had selected for his last resting place.

In the year of his death, on February 12, 1794, Steuben had made provision as to the distribution of his property. The original of this last will is among the "Steuben Papers" in the New York Historical Society. It reads as follows:

"I, Frederick William Baron de Steuben of the City and State of New York do make this my last will and testament.

Sufficient reasons having determined me to exclude my relations in Europe from any participation in my estate in America and to adopt my Friends and former Aid De Camps Benjamin Walker and William North as my children and make them sole devisees of all my estates therein, except as herein-afterwards is otherwise disposed of in consequence thereof.

I bequeath to the said Benjamin Walker the sum of Three Thousand dollars, and the Gold hilted sword given to me by Congress.

To the said William North I bequeath my silver hilted sword and the gold box given me by the City of New York.

To John I. Mulligan I bequeath the whole of my Library, Maps and Charts, and the sum of Two Thousand five hundred Dollars to complete it,

And to each of my Servants living with me at the time of my decease one year's wages and besides this to my valet de chambre all my wearing apparel; but I do hereby declare that those legacies to my Servants are on the following conditions; that on my decease they do not permit any person to touch my Body, nor even to change the shirt, in which I shall die, but that they wrap me up in my old Military Cloak and in twenty-four hours after my Decease bury me in such spot as I shall before my Decease point out to them, and that they never acquaint any person with the place where I shall be buried.

And lastly I do give, devise and bequeath all the rest and residue of my Estate real and Personal after the Payment of my Debts and the legacies aforesaid to the said Benjamin Walker and William North, to hold to them their Heirs, Executors and Administrators share and share alike hereby appointing the said Benjamin Walker & William North Executors of this my last Will and Testament and revoking all former Wills by me heretofore made.

New York February 12 1794.

Steuben. (L. S.)

A few more words must be said about Steuben's burial place. When in later years a wagon road was laid out through this part of the country, running directly over the grave, Walker had the remains of Steuben removed farther into the woods. To prevent any further desecration he donated fifty acres of the woodland to a Baptist Society in the neighborhood, with the stipulation, that five acres of this forest, including Steuben's grave, must be kept fenced forever and uncleared, and that no cattle or other animals should be permitted therein.

This second grave was marked with a stone slab, which in 1870 was replaced by a suitable monument of granite, provided for by German organizations throughout the United States. The cornerstone of this monument, which is a massive structure, 14 feet square and 15 feet high, was laid June 1, 1870, by Governor Seymour in the presence of thousands of people. The ceremony opened with the old Prussian national hymn, played by a military band. After an eloquent address, Governor Seymour laid the stone with these words:

"In behalf of our German fellow citizens, in behalf of the citizens of the State of New York, in behalf of the whole American people, who desire that the mem-

Tomb of Baron von Steuben in Oneida County, N. Y.
From a Drawing by Rudolf Cronau.

ory of this great man shall never pass away, since his Revolutionary acts were instrumental in laying the corner stone of our liberties, I now deposit the corner stone of this monument, erected in honor of the memory of Baron Frederick William Steuben. May God grant that it will ever serve to remind the American people of the great service which he performed in their cause, which he adopted as his own. May God grant that it may always be treasured as sacredly as we treasure his memory to-day."

An address was given by Mr. Sixtus Karl Kapff in behalf of the New York German Society, whose members were present in large numbers. An ode "Das ist der Tag des Herrn" was sung by members of the New York Liederkranz, after which another American soldier of German extraction, General Franz Sigel, made an address in German.

The monument was unveiled in summer, 1872.

Some years ago the author of this book paid homage here to the memory of his great countryman. All traces of Steuben's log-cabin had disappeared. But a part of the primeval forest was still there, a remainder of the immense wilderness, that before the coming of the white man stretched as far as the Mississippi river. Seen from the distance, the arched silhouette of this grove reminded one strongly of these huge mounds, which in ancient times were heaped in northern Germany, Denmark and Scandinavia over the sepulchres of famous heroes. Entering the mysterious twilight of this grove, the visitor soon discovers the monument. The simple name "Steuben," surrounded by a wreath of oakleaves, indicates who holds here his eternal rest. The trunks and branches of fallen trees, overgrown with moss and fern, cover the ground. According to Steuben's wish they must not be removed as they preach that transitoriness which governs all things in nature.

Posthumus Honors and Appreciations.

Of the many tributes of honor extended to the character of Steuben and to his work, those are of especial value rendered by men who were in frequent contact with him. In what high regard Steuben was held by Washington, appears from the many letters which he as commander-in-chief wrote in Steuben's behalf as well as from the fact that the Baron was his guest very frequently during Washington's stay in New York as President.

But no appreciations are more touching than those given by William North, Steuben's former aide-de-camp. Having shared for seven years all the hardships and miseries of the war, each one had learned to value the excellent character of the other. In time this feeling waxed into such close friendship, that death only could part them. There are many proofs of the deep respect in which Steuben was held by North. When in 1786 Major North was ordered to the Ohio country, to establish there a fort and a settlement, he named the fort after his former chief. It was situated were to-day the flourishing city Steubenville stands.

How deeply affected North was by Steuben's death, we can judge by the inscription of a memorial tablet, he had placed in Steuben's memory upon the walls of the German Reformed Church, then in Nassau Street, New York City. In later years this monument was transferred into the German Evangelical Reformed Church at 355 East 68th Street. It has the following inscription:

Sacred to the Memory of
Frederick William August Baron Steuben
a German
Knight of the Order of Fidelity;
Aide-de-Camp to Frederick the Great, King of Prussia;
Major-General & Inspector General

in the Revolutionary War.
Esteemed, respected and supported by Washington,
he gave military Skill & Discipline
to the Citizen-Soldiers;
who,
(fulfilling the Decrees of Heaven),
achieved the Independence of the United States.
The highly polished manners of the Baron
were graced
by the most noble feelings of the heart.
His hand, "open as day for melting Charity,"
closed only in the strong grasp of Death.
This Memorial is inscribed
by an American
who had the honor to be his Aide-de-Camp,
the happiness to be his Friend.
Obiit 1794

There is still another proof for the deep reverence Wm. North held towards his departed chief. Some time before his own death, which occurred in 1836, at the age of 81 years, he sat down and wrote a sketch of Steuben's life. Since Steuben's departure forty years had passed, nevertheless the freshness of this sketch indicates how deeply many incidents had impressed themselves on the mind of the young man, while he assisted him as an aide-de-camp.

This sketch has been printed in the Magazine of American history, March, 1882, pages 187-199.

Pierre Etienne Duponceau, a young Frenchman who came over with Steuben from Europe as his secretary, and remained with him till fall 1780, wrote the following lines:

"He was much beloved by the soldiers, though he was a strict disciplinarian. But there was in him a fund of goodness which displayed itself on many occasions, and which could even be read in his severe countenance, so that he was extremely popular."

The historian, George Bancroft said of Steuben:
"The memory of Steuben has many claims upon the

present generation. To the cause of our country in the times of its distress he, at the sacrifice of a secure career, devoted the experience and skill which had been the fruit of long years of service under the greatest master of the art of war of that day. He rendered the inestimable benefit of introducing a better rule into the discipline of the American Army and stricter accountability in the distribution of military stores. He served under our flag with implicit fidelity, with indefatigable industry, and a courage that shrunk from no danger. His presence was important both in the camp and on the field of battle, from the huts of Valley Forge to Yorktown, and he remained with us till his death."

On May 22, 1902, Richard Bartholdt, of Missouri,

RICHARD BARTHOLDT

introduced in the House of Representatives a bill for the erection of a statue to the memory of Baron Steuben at Washington, D. C., and that the sum of $50,000 should be appropriated for this purpose. The bill was adopted and approved in February, 1903, whereon competition was invited for such a statue. It resulted in the selection of a model, submitted by Albert Jaegers of New York, born 1868 in Elberfeld, Germany. It was decided, to erect this monument at the northwest corner of Lafayette Square, opposite the White House, the same ground in which already the statues of Lafayette, Rochambeau and Kosciuszko had been placed.

The statue of Steuben was unveiled on December 7, 1910. After a ringing chorus by nearly a thousand voices of the "Nordöstliche Sängerbund von Amerika" (Northeastern Singer's Association) speeches were delivered by Representative Bartholdt, Dr. Charles Hexamer, President of the "National German-American Alliance" and the German ambassador, Count J. H. von Bernstorff. Then the statue was unveiled by Miss Helen Taft, daughter of President Taft. At the same time the singing societies, accompanied by the Marine Band, sang "The Star Spangled Banner." After a salute by Battery E of the Third Field Artillery had been fired, President Taft spoke in praise of Von Steuben. He said:

"The effect of Steuben's instruction in the American Army teaches us a lesson that it is well for us all to keep in mind, and that is that no people, however warlike in spirit and ambition, in natural courage and self-confidence, can be made at once, by uniforms and guns, a military force. Until they learn drill and discipline, they are a mob, and the theory than they can be made an army overnight has cost this Nation billions of dollars and thousands of lives.

"The history of Von Steuben's services shows him a kindly, considerate, brave, and accomplished soldier. As Inspector General, his achievements were not the successes of an independent command, but they were the preparation by persistent but tedious drilling and discipline of men to serve effectively under other commanders and to win for them victory. It seemed a thankless task, for it had none of the spectacular in it, none of the glory of military triumph. It was the basic hard work without which such triumphs could not be won, but the results inured to the glory of others.

"Steuben asked for no reward, except that if his services were satisfactory, at the end of the war he should be recompensed for the sacrifices he had made in leaving his home and giving up lucrative rank and office. Washington, that calm, sane, just judge of men, recognized fully the debt that he and the army and the people owed to Von Steuben, and it is gratifying to know that he gave his evidence as he laid down his command of the Army in a letter full of expressions of gratitude to his comrade in arms, whose important aid at a critical juncture he fully appreciated.

"When Baron Steuben came to this country he found Germans who had preceded him, and who, like him, had elected to make this their permanent home. Since his day millions of his countrymen have come to be Americans, and it adds great interest to our celebration and emphasizes the propriety of the action of Congress in erecting this statue to know that the German race since the Revolution has made so large a part of our population and played so prominent a part in the great growth and development of our country. It is particularly appropriate that there is present the German ambassador, the personal representative of the illustrious successor of Frederick the Great. The Germans who have become American citizens and their descendants may well take pride in this occasion and in this work of art, modeled by the hand of an American of German descent, which commemorates the valued contribution made by a German soldier to the cause of American freedom at the time of its birth."

Following the President's address, the benediction was pronounced by Rev. Dr. Wm. Russell; and a military and civic parade then started. It was reviewed by the President and special guests. There were about 10,000 men in line.

During the evening a banquet at the Army and Navy Club united a large number of members of the Order of the Cincinnati, which had gathered from all parts of the country to do honor to the founder of this oldest and most distinguished of the hereditary societies in the United States.

Following the sculptor's description of the monument the figure of Steuben, 11 feet high, appears standing on an eminence inspecting the great maneuvers of 1778. He is heavily cloaked as if to endure the hardships of the rigorous winter campaign at Valley Forge. The sash is reminiscent of his service on the staff of Frederick the Great. His hand lightly at rest on the hilt of his sword, he is following with keen interest the unfolding movement of the troops.

The two sides of the monument show beautiful groups, the one "Military instruction" represents Steuben's life work, the work for which this Nation honors and remembers him—the drilling and training of the American Army. An experienced warrior is shown instructing a youth in the use of the sword.

In the second group, "Commemoration," America is teaching youth to honor the memory of her heroes. A foreign branch is grafted into the tree of her national life. She welds to her heart the foreigner who has cast his life and fortune with the weal and woe of her people, embodying the idea of unity and fraternity of all nationalities under the guidance of a great Republic.

The reverse of the monument is adorned with a rectangular medallion, showing portraits of Steuben's faithful aides and friends, Col. North and Benj. Walker.

A replica of the statue of Steuben was in 1912 presented by the Government of the United States to the German Emperor and the German nation in return for the statue of Frederick the Great. As the site for this replica Potsdam, the favorite home and resting place of Frederick the Great was selected. The statue was presented on behalf of the United States by Hon. Richard Bartholdt, the Representative of Missouri in Congress, and by Charles B. Wolffram of New York City. The solemn unveiling of the monument took place in the presence of the Emperor on August 5, 1912.

Statue of Major General Von Steuben in Washington. D. C.
Modeled by Albert Jaegers.

"In Times of Peace Prepare for War"—the Great But Unheeded Lesson of Steuben's Life.

The eventful life of Steuben teaches a lesson which was well understood and proclaimed by Washington, but utterly ignored by all his successors. In a former chapter it has been stated that Steuben, foreseeing the possibility of further conflicts with England or other foreign powers, declared that it would be wise in times of peace to prepare for war, that therefore every citizen ought to be trained in the use of arms and ready for the defense of his country, and that a regular army should be created.

When on January 8, 1790, President Washington delivered in person his first address before Congress at the opening of its second session, his first recommendation related to a provision for the common defense by a proper military establishment. He repeated Steuben's admonition in the following sentence: "To be prepared for War is one of the most effectual means of preserving peace!"

Provision was made for a regular army, but it was inadequate and far behind the expectations of the President as well as of Steuben and other patriotic men. There still lingered in the minds of the representatives of the people the unreasonable opposition against all things military, which fails to discriminate between an army billeted on the people, and an army springing from the people, retaining their high ideals and obedient to their will.

Under the heading "A Discussion of National Defense" the "Saturday Evening Post" of March 10, 1923, published an article by General John Pershing, in which he said:

"Glancing over the history of our republic, we find that experience has not wholly eradicated the prejudice against all things military. In the Revolutionary War the colonies, obviously compelled to create armies to fight their battles, encountered difficulties that should have indicated the wisdom of some provision for future defense. Yet the suffering and cost were soon forgotten, even by actual participants; opposition remained, and the counsel given by Washington himself, after forty-five years of public service, that the way to prevent war was to be prepared to meet the enemy, went unheeded, and, for that matter, it has practically remained so up to our day.

"The War of 1812 found the young nation sailing along apparently without thought that armies might again be needed, at least so far as any rational measures to the contrary would indicate. The matter of national defense was left to the several states; but the means adopted for the support and training of the militia were half- hearted and various, any plan of uniformity being generally resisted by the states. Entry into the war was accompanied by trumpets and oratory, but the conduct of the forces can be recorded only with humiliation. Even the capital was left defenseless, only to be captured and burned by a handful of British. Our troops were untrained and everywhere badly handled, and, of course, fled before the enemy from nearly every field.

"The blame for this disgraceful showing could have been laid to the faulty system, yet nobody seems to have thought much about it one way or the other. Not only were no new steps taken afterwards to organize the citizen forces against a similar emergency but the remaining small regular force was immediately reduced to almost nothing."

Reviewing the Civil War, Pershing states that the earlier battles were fought by partially trained troops, that after the close of the war, the Army was again reduced to a mere skeleton, and that advocates of sensible precaution against another war were heard only as those crying in the wilderness.

Coming down to the Spanish War, Pershing says: "We again suffered from the resulting extravagant efforts to overcome previous stupidity and neglect, and the unnecessary loss of life in unsanitary camps is shocking to remember."

About America's plunge into the World War Pershing makes the following severe remarks: "All we can say is that through these years we, the people and those who make our laws, have gone from bad to worse, learning little, doing less, still prejudiced, lullel into inaction by an unwarranted sense of security and by false ideas of economy, instead of using plain, practical common sense and making reasonable provision in time of peace for the maintenance of a moderate policy of national defense.

"Let us now briefly review our situation in 1917. First of all, we had only a small Regular Army scattered in groups throughout the country, and the National Guard was only partially organized. The Draft Law had to be hastily drawn and put into execution to meet the demand for men. There were only 14,000 regular and partially trained National Guard officers combined, while 150,000 would be needed. Newly appointed civilian officers had to be given hurried courses and sent to train troops. It was necessary to build cantonments at tremendous expense for the concentration of millions of recruits for instruction. Organizations had to be worked out for all units of our Armies. Welfare workers were required to meet new conditions of life among these men, massed as they were in large camps. In the confusion contingents of men were ordered about like misdirected mail, one group being sent from the Atlantic to the Pacific and almost immediately back again. All railroads were congested by the excessive movements of troops, material and supplies.

"As to the artillery, there was none to speak of, and the French had to furnish us enough for thirty divisions. One of the first contracts made in France was for $60,000,000 worth of airplanes. Our tanks were obtained from the French, but only in very limited numbers. As to sea transportation, wooden ships were built and condemned, concrete ships were launched and sunk, and steel ships became a question of recklessly paid riveters. Many classes of supplies simply did not exist, as the Allies had already cleaned out our storehouses on long-term contracts before we entered the war. Competition in procurement among different government agencies, even as to labor, became so widespread and so extravagant that it amounted to a scandal. As a direct consequence of our unwise pettiness in the years of peace the Government's expenditures in 1918 reached a volume of $2,000,000 an hour."

Speaking about "the wickedness of unpreparedness" Pershing furthermore says: "The cause of almost every difficulty of the soldier and the Government developed in the World War can be traced directly to our woeful lack of preparation."

Discussing the different means of coast defense at the disposal of the Government, Pershing explains that the navy is really useless without a supporting merchant marine. "Could anything be more pathetic than the historic cruise of our fleet around the world, supplied by chartered vessels flying British and other foreign flags? We spent billions for the construction of ships during the war, yet more than half our troops were transported in foreign bottoms. Our exports and our tourists are carried principally in foreign ships. Blindly provincial, we pay for the support of foreign merchant marine, give other nations a mandate over the seas, and still continue to expect this country to occupy a commanding position in the world of trade and other international relations."

Many people who read these criticisms may regard them as unduly severe. But those who were compelled to investigate the many scandals connected with the mobilization of the American Army in 1917, must admit that these verdicts are merely intimations of an almost unbelievable inefficiency and corruption.

From a similar article, written by Lieutenant Colonel W. Jefferson Davis and printed in the New York American of Sunday, May 27, 1923, the following lines may be quoted:

"In aviation we have done more individually and less nationally than perhaps any important country in the world. We have broken most records, and then let our airplane factories go to smash. We have made vital discoveries, and are sending most of our equipment to rust.

"As a people we are intensely interested in aviation. As a nation we act as though it were a remote, impracticable, visionary project to be slightly encouraged by the bestowal of benign benedictions unaccompanied by appropriations.

"It probably is utterly useless to preach preparedness to America. We are so confoundedly unmilitary that, left to our own devices, the extent of our warlike preparations would perhaps be a pair of boxing gloves —a most excellent trait if it were shared by the rest of the world, but unfortunately even the most optimistic peace lovers have ceased proclaiming that the world has seen its last war.

"No one hopes more earnestly than I do that America may never be called upon to fire another gun; but I do not believe it. I think few students of world conditions believe it. However, I do not believe in preparing for war, but I do most sternly believe in preparing for self-defense."

"Again America needs another Steuben!" exclaimed the late Professor Marion Dexter Learned of the Pennsylvania University. "and again it is Prussia which can teach us both by precept and example. Instead of indulging in ignorant harangues about "German militarism," "Prussianism" and the like, it behooves us to study the merits of this marvellous military machine in all its minutest details and once more learn from our great preceptor, Germany, this supreme lesson of national defense.

"The great imitable factors in the German system are universal military service, thorough organization, absolute articulation of military and civic agencies in national defense—all principles as chaotic relatively in America at the present time as they were in the days of Steuben at Valley Forge. If America were called upon to answer to the roll of civilized nations in military fitness, it is doubtful whether we should not stand last on the list of actual efficiency—even after little

Montenegro. This is a crime which none can condone, a sin against our traditions, an outrage against the instincts of humanity. It is high time that America had a military organization, which should study incessantly the methods of modern warfare, and an advisory or adjunct Civic Council, which should represent all the industrial, economic, social and scientific activities of the nation, and cooperate with the great central military and naval department of the Government in coordinating all these interests in a self-adjusting system of National defense."*

* German-American Annals 1916.

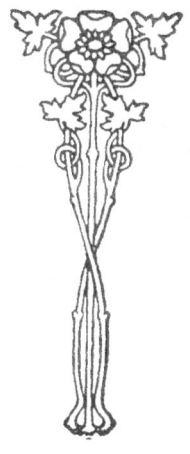

The Steuben Society of America and Its Aims.

When the 20th century was ushered in, there were strong indications, that for the German element in the United States a new and promising era was beginning. Alive to the great advantages of centralization a small number of representative citizens of various States of the Union, among them the author of this book, assembled in Philadelphia, to organize a National German-American Alliance, not for the purpose of forming a State within the States, but to consolidate the enormous forces of the German-American element for the sole purpose of promoting everything that is good in German character and culture, and that might accrue to the benefit and welfare of the whole American nation.

The constituting convention took place on October 6, 1901, in the hall of the German Society of Pennsylvania and was combined with a celebration of the "German Day" in commemoration of the landing of the German Pilgrims in Philadelphia on October 6, 1683. The platform adopted in this convention contained nothing whatever that is not in full accord with loyal citizenship and the best interests of the whole country. In recognition of this fact, the Alliance was, after a painstaking investigation of its aims and purposes, incorporated on February 27, 1907, by an Act of Congress.

In accordance with its principles, the German-American Alliance promoted the culture of gymnastics, song, music, art, literature and the study of foreign languages. By lifting its members from the narrow limits of club life, it induced them to acquire the right of citizenship as soon as they were legally entitled to it, in order that they participate in all affairs of public life. Through its committees it made recommendations for the preservation and wise utilization of all natural resources of our country. And by founding Junior Orders it seeks to inspire the younger generation to continue the good work of their fathers, and to display the same industriousness, enterprise and patriotism. And so it strove in many directions to win recognition for its motto: "Always true to our adopted country; ever ready to risk all for its welfare; respecting the law, and sincere and unselfish in the duties of citizenship."

Unfortunately the World War, caused by British envy and French hate and resulting in such frightful destruction of lives and property, overthrew also the good work of the German-American Alliance. British and French propaganda, invading every American newspaper, home, school, college, university, church, stage and cinema, poisoned public opinion to the core. No citizen dared trust his own friends. Violence, bloodshed and murder began to run amuck. The press did yeoman's duty in the suppression of free speech, liberty and other human rights. The clergy and many members of the bar combined in efforts to lash aversion into a state of hate and maniacal fury. Congressmen and Senators, not wishing to lag behind, adopted on May 4, 1918, the detestable Espionage Act, thereby creating a system of terrorism, which assumed most threatening aspects when the Attorney General called for 200,000 volunteers to act as agents of the Department of Justice to report all persons suspected of being "pro-German."

The chairman of the Judiciary Committee of the U. S. Senate, Wm. H. King of Utah, who perhaps had never before heard of the German-American Alliance, became obsessed by the idea that he might win everlasting fame by smashing this most dangerous institution ever created by the peace-loving German element in America. Accordingly he introduced a bill to repeal the charter of the National German-American Alliance. As there was no hope for justice from such prejudiced enemies the board of directors of the German-American Alliance decided to dissolve voluntarily. This was done on April 13 1918, a month before the charter was repealed. The funds of the Alliance, amounting to

$30,000, were turned over to the American Red Cross.

At that time the author of this book, one of the founders of the German-American Alliance, was president of the Bronx County branch of the society. When the will of the board of directors became known, he submitted to the members of the branch the proposition, to continue in the good work and regular meetings, but to form a new society, for which he suggested, to indicate its strictly loyal character, the names "George Washington League," or "Steuben Society." But a majority of the members, discouraged by the hostile attitude of the Government toward everything German voted for postponement. So this matter rested till spring 1919, when it was brought up again by the writer in several friendly meetings with a number of gentlemen, all from New York.

They were: Dr. Franz Koempel, S. de Lange, Rudolf Pagenstecher, Theodor Haebler, George Riefflin, Professor Edmund von Mach, Gustav Lindenthal, Edmund Stirn, Dr. J. Bullinger, Dr. Frank, H. R. Habicht, Professor Walz, Dr. A. Busse, Dr. C. Kayser, Wm. Funk, Frederick F. Schrader, and others.

Finally, these meetings resulted in founding of the STEUBEN SOCIETY OF AMERICA, an organization of American citizens of German descent in honor and commemoration of the maker of the American Army.

The Society's Creed is:

ONE COUNTRY—A country so fair, tolerant and just that all who live in it, may love it.

ONE FLAG—An American flag for American purposes only.

ONE LANGUAGE—The language of TRUTH spoken in any tongue in which one chooses to speak it.

The aims and purposes of this Society are:

Loyally to support the Constitution of the United States of America.

To aid in maintaining the independence and sovereignty of the United States and its freedom from foreign influence.

To establish co-operation among its members in the

exercise of their civic duties, and to encourage among them an active participation in every phase of national life.

To promote the intellectual, social and material wellbeing of its members and their fellow citizens.

To disseminate as widely as possible knowledge of the great achievements of citizens of German stock in the development of our country;

To bring about the complete rehabilitation of the Germanic element in the United States, politically, socially and economically, and its universal recognition as an integral part of our citizenry on the basis of absolute equality in all things.

The nation-wide movement inaugurated by The Steuben Society of America is not separatistic in any sense. The Society is thoroughly American in character, citizens of the United States exclusively participating in its activities. It is not striving to secure special privileges for the racial element it represents, or to perpetuate ill-feeling engendered during the war, or keep open the wounds caused by hatred, misrepresentation, intolerance and tyrannical oppression. On the contrary, it purposes to obliterate the painful past as quickly as possible, heal the wounds left by the war, and assist in re-establishing that harmonious, neighborly co-operation and feeling of solidarity among the various racial elements of our composite population which existed before the World War, and without which our great republic can not endure or successfully fulfill its great mission among the nations of the world.

On motion of the writer, September 17th, the day of Steuben's birth was adopted as "STEUBEN DAY." to be celebrated every year with patriotic speeches and other entertainments fit for such an occasion.

The first of such commemoration was held in 1922 in the auditorium of Morris High School, Bronx, N. Y. Attended by more than 1500 members it was in every respect a full success.

As "STEUBEN DAY" will be observed by all units of the Society, the prediction Joseph B. Doyle, the historian of the "National Society of the Sons of the American Revolution" has made in his splendid book on Steuben, will become true: "Like Hamilton in the Revolution and Stanton in the Civil War, Steuben's character seems to expand as men begin more and more to appreciate the quality of the man, the work he was called upon to perform, and the difficulties he encountered in performing it. Posterity is beginning to realize what his contemporaries could not fully comprehend, and while many a prominent character of that day has been forgotten or only mentioned as a sort of connecting link in the endless chain of events, Steuben looms up more and more as the perspective lengthens. As the disinterested patriot, as the skillful disciplinarian, as the able general, as the confidant, the adviser and the friend of Washington, as the honest and thorough gentleman, he proved himself a worthy compeer of those great characters who laid the foundations for this republic so deep and strong that it has successfully withstood the whirlwinds of a century and a quarter, the strain of war and the laxity of peace, the struggle with adversity and the more insidious enervation as the result of prosperity."

Fullname Index

ADAMS, 125 John 121
ALLEN, Lt 61-62
ANDERSON, John 59-60
ANDRE, 60-61 67 John 59 Maj 57
ARBUTHNOT, Adm 74
ARMSTRONG, J 117 John 93
ARNOLD, 59-62 67-68 B 63 66 Benedict 57-58 73-74
ASHLIN, Lee 13
BADEN, Magrave Of 2
BANCROFT, George 134
BARTHOLDT, Representative 136 Richard 135 138
BERNSTORFF, J H Von 136
BOYER, Ludwig 108
BULLINGER, J 148
BURGOYNE, 34
BUSSE, A 148
CHANNING, 58
CLINTON, 38 49 73 125 Henry 48 58-59 63-64 67 Sir 66
COCHRANE, Col 104 Mrs 104
CONWAY, Thomas 28
CORNWALLIS, 77-80 85 Lord 76
CRONAU, Rudolf 131
DAVIS, W Jefferson 143
DEANE, Silas 3
DENMARK, King Of 2
DOYLE, Joseph 40 149

DUANE, James 117
DUER, Chancellor 117
DUPONCEAU, 1 15 M 40 Pierre 134
EARLE, Ralph 10
ESPINIERES, De 1
EUGENE, Prince Of Austria 70
FLEURY, Col 40
FRANCE, King Of 2
FRANK, Dr 148
FRANKLIN, 4 30 Benjamin 3
FREDERICK, King Of Prussia 133 The Great 1 4-5 10 37 45 108 137-138
FUNK, Wm 148
GARDEN, Alexander 54
GATES, 80 Gen 33 64 69 93 117
GEORGE, King Of Great Britain 29 96 103
GERMAIN, George 62 Lord 66
GIBBONS, Lt 84
GRASSE, Adm De 77
GREENE, 73 95 Ashbel 10 Gen 19 32 57 71-72 76 86 Nathaniel 47 71
HABICHT, H R 148
HAEBLER, Theodor 148
HALDIMAND, Gen 103
HAMILTON, 150 Alexander 35 117 Col 19

HANCOCK, John 7 Mr 6
HAND, Gen 100
HATFIELD, J T 5
HEADLEY, J T 94
HEATH, Gen 100-101
HEER, Bartholomaeus Von 37
   Maj Von 108
HEXAMER, Charles 136
HOCHBAUM, Elfrieda 5
HOHENZOLLERN-
   HECHINGEN, Prince Of 2
HOWE, 34 Gen 7-8 47 57
   Robert 71 William 33 37
JAEGERS, Albert 136 139
JAMESON, Col 61
JAY, John 117 127
JEFFERSON, Thomas 72
JOHNSON, Col 50
JONES, Pomeroy 67
KALB, De 39 Gen De 31 69
KAPFF, Sixtus 132
KAPP, Friedrich 40
KAYSER, C 148
KING, Wm 147
KNOX, 95 125 Gen 14 47 80
   100-101 105 114 Henry 112
KOEMPEL, Franz 148
KOSCIUSZKO, 136
L'ENFANT, De 1 40 Maj 102
LAFAYETTE, 31 39 74 76-77
   136 Gen 62 80 Marquis De
   79 120
LANGE, S De 148
LAURENS, Col 19 28 Mr 9
LAWSON, Gen 72 74
LEARNED, Marion Dexter 144
LEE, 33-34 36-37 Arthur 3
   Charles 32 Gen 35 38
LINCOLN, Benjamin 111 Gen
   80
LINDENTHAL, Gustav 148
LIVINGSTON, 125 Chancellor
   117 Robert 59

MACH, Edmund Von 148
MCMASTER, 116 Bach 29
MEYTINGER, Col 108 Jacob 37
MONTMORENCY, Marquis De
   83
MOORE, George 37
MUEHLENBERG, 77 Gen 74
   Peter 72
MUHLENBERG, Frederick 121
MULLIGAN, J W 126 John 128-
   129
MUTTER, Johann 37
NICOLA, Lewis 87
NORTH, 55 Col 84 Maj 104 128
   William 23 79 118 129-130
   Wm 53 83 88 91 126 134
OTIS, 125
PAGE, John 118
PAGENSTECHER, Rudolf 148
PAINE, Thomas 8
PAULDING, 61
PERSHING, 141-143 John 140
PETERS, Richard 54 97
PONTIERE, De 1
PRUSSIA, King Of 5-6 9
PUTNAM, 95
RIEFFLIN, George 148
ROBINSON, 60 62 Beverly 59
ROCHAMBEAU, 77 136 Gen
   De 59
ROMANAI, De 1
RUSSELL, Wm 137
SAINTCLAIR, 125
SAINTGERMAIN, Count 2
SAINTGERMAINE, 4
SCAMMEL, A 23
SCHRADER, Frederick 5 148
SCHUYLER, Philip 59
SCHWEIZER, J Otto 20
SEYMOUR, Gov 130
SHAW, Capt 100
SHEAF, 126
SHERMAN, 125

SHIPPEN, Judge 58 Margaret 58
SIGEL, Franz 132
SMITH, 61 Col 115 Joshua 60
STAGG, Capt 114
STANTON, 150
STEUBEN, 2 4-8 10 12 15 18-26 28-29 32 35-40 45-46 50 53-55 67 69-74 76-80 83-85 87-91 95 97-101 103-104 108 110-115 117-118 122-123 125-128 130 132 134 137-138 140 144 146 148-150 Baron 9 41 47 120 136 Baron De 30-31 107 Baron Von 106 Frederick William 132 Frederick William August 133 Frederick William Baron De 129 Frederick William De 121 Friedrich Wilhelm Von 1 Jonathan 68 Maj Gen Von 139
STEWART, Col 85
STIRLING, Gen 31 Lord 32
STIRN, Edmund 148
STRUEBING, Philipp 37
SULLIVAN, 95 John 23
TAFT, Helen 136

TALLMADGE, Benjamin 105 Maj 61
TERNANT, Jean Baptiste 85
THATCHER, Dr 104 John 84
TRUMBALL, John 81
TRUMBULL, John 11
VAUGHAN, Gen 49
VERPLANCK, 99
WALKER, 24 B 118 Benjamin 55 115 126 129-130 Capt 36 40 Col 128
WALZ, Prof 148
WASHINGTON, 7 10 19 21 29-30 32-35 37-39 48 54 57 59 61-62 67 69 71 74 77-78 80 83 85 87-89 92-96 99 101 103 105-106 108 110-111 116 126 134 141 150 G 121 Gen 8-9 28 31 50 63-64 George 6 11 47 125 148 Go 107 Mrs 126 President 140
WAYNE, 80 95 Anthony 49-50 Gen 57 79 Mad Anthony 49
WEEDON, Gen 76
WHITE, 128
WILLIAM, Frederick 68
WILLIAMS, Otho 83
WOLFFRAM, Charles 138

153

Other Heritage Books by Don Heinrich Tolzmann:

Amana: William Rufus Perkins' and Barthinius L. Wick's History of the Amana Society, or Community of True Inspiration

Americana Germanica: Paul Ben Baginsky's Bibliography of German Works Relating to America, 1493-1800

Biography of Baron Von Steuben, the Army of the American Revolution and Its Organizer: Rudolf Cronau's Biography of Baron von Steuben

CD: German-American Biographical Index (Midwest Families)

CD: Germans, Volume 2

CD: The German Colonial Era (four volumes)

Cincinnati's German Heritage

Covington's German Heritage

Custer: Frederick Whittaker's Complete Life of General George A. Custer, Major General of Volunteers, Brevet Major General U.S. Army and Lieutenant-Colonel Seventh U.S. Cavalry

Dayton's German Heritage: Karl Karstaedt's Golden Jubilee History of the German Pioneer Society of Dayton, Ohio

Early German-American Newspapers: Daniel Miller's History

German Americans in the Revolution

German Immigration to America: The First Wave

German Pioneer Life and Domestic Customs

German Pioneer Lifestyle

German Pioneers in Early California: Erwin G. Gudde's History

German-American Achievements: 400 Years of Contributions to America

German-Americana: A Bibliography

Germany and America, 1450-1700

Kentucky's German Pioneers: H.A. Rattermann's History

Lives and Exploits of the Daring Frank and Jesse James: Thaddeus Thorndike's Graphic and Realistic Description of Their Many Deeds of Unparalleled Daring in the Robbing of Banks and Railroad Trains

Louisiana's German Heritage: Louis Voss' Introductory History

Maryland's German Heritage: Daniel Wunderlich Nead's History

Memories of the Battle of New Ulm: Personal Accounts of the Sioux Uprising. L. A. Fritsche's History of Brown County, Minnesota (1916)

Michigan's German Heritage: John Andrew Russell's History of the German Influence in the Making of Michigan

Ohio's German Heritage

Outbreak and Massacre by the Dakota Indians in Minnesota in 1862: Marion P. Satterlee's Minute Account of the Outbreak, with Exact Locations, Names of All Victims, Prisoners at Camp Release, Refugees at Fort Ridgely, etc. Complete List of Indians Killed in Battle and Those Hung, and Those Pardoned at Rock Island, Iowa

The German Element in Virginia: Herrmann Schuricht's History

The German Immigrant in America

The Pennsylvania Germans: James Owen Knauss, Jr.'s Social History

The Pennsylvania Germans: Jesse Leonard Rosenberger's Sketch of Their History and Life

www.ingramcontent.com/pod-product-compliance
Lightning Source LLC
Chambersburg PA
CBHW050638160426
43194CB00010B/1725